# ONE WAS NOT ENOUGH

*True Stories of Multiple Murderers*

D0681154

# One Was Not Enough

## *True Stories of Multiple Murderers*

by

### GEORGINA LLOYD

**BANTAM BOOKS**
TORONTO · NEW YORK · LONDON · SYDNEY · AUCKLAND

# ONE WAS NOT ENOUGH
## A BANTAM BOOK 0 553 17605 6

Originally published in Great Britain by Robert Hale Ltd.

PRINTING HISTORY
Robert Hale edition published 1986
Bantam Books edition published 1989
Bantam Books edition reprinted 1992
Bantam Books edition reprinted 1993

Bantam Books are published by Transworld Publishers Ltd., 61–63 Uxbridge Road, Ealing, London W5 5SA, in Australia by Transworld Publishers (Australia) Pty. Ltd., 15–25 Helles Avenue, Moorebank, NSW 2170, and in New Zealand by Transworld Publishers (N.Z.) Ltd., 3 William Pickering Drive, Albany, Auckland.

Printed and bound in Great Britain by Cox & Wyman Ltd., Reading, Berks.

# CONTENTS

# Introduction

The forensic psychiatrist is often asked by the police whether he can describe the type of person they should be looking for when a series of murders has been committed. This is especially important when the murders are sadistic or sexual. The better the description, according to police thinking, the greater the likelihood of early detection and arrest before someone else becomes a victim.

Unfortunately however, there is no particular 'type of person' who commits multiple murder. For example, contrary to popular imagination, he is not necessarily of low intelligence or overtly aggressive. Neither is he a hulking brute, nor does he necessarily have a police record or have been a mental patient. Outwardly, if not inwardly, he can look as normal as the rest of us. He can be tall or short, fat or thin, young or old, educated or illiterate.

Some of these men may be loners who cannot make friends easily, but this is not invariably the case. However, a goodly percentage of such men are withdrawn and introspective, avoiding company and preferring solitary pursuits such as reading, music and the cinema or watching television. He may appear shy and retiring, reserved and quiet, even well-mannered and polite, showing no outward sign of the turmoil within his disordered mind.

Because this type of person rarely, if ever, reacts to violence and avoids fighting even at school, it is often hard to believe that he could be a suspect. In this way he is often able to avoid bringing suspicion upon himself for long periods of time. He may have obsessional traits, and evidence of these can sometimes be noted at the scene of a crime, for example, a victim's shoes placed neatly side by side. Such a man will himself be meticulous about his own personal appearance.

Not uncommonly the multiple murderer feels different from others and insecure because of his isolation. Occasionally these feelings are sensed by his associates who may consider him to be a bit of a 'weirdo' and tend therefore to avoid his company. This, of course, reinforces his sense of isolation.

Sometimes he feels inferior and the planning of his murders may make him feel superior to other men in compensation. In extreme cases, others then become to him inferior beings to be used in any way he wishes without regard to their rights as fellow humans. The psychopath is particularly liable to commit acts of violence after he has suffered a loss of his self-esteem or his masculinity has been challenged. Often he feels he is clever enough to outwit the police, and reading of his own notoriety in the newspapers will be such a boost to his ego that he will continue his outrages. Some such killers send letters about their own crimes to the police and to newspapers.

The sadistic serial murderer is typically a daydreamer with an active fantasy life, often peopled by bizarre beings, or focused on Nazi atrocities and similar imaginings. As a child he may have been noticeably seen to be 'living in a dream world' which was often more real to him than the actual world around him. It is fortunate indeed for society that the vast majority of sadistic psychopaths restrict their activities to fantasizing in the recesses of their darkened minds and do not act out these horrific fantasies . . .

But those who do frequently return home after the crime and behave normally, eating and sleeping, going to work, conversing with fellow beings. This is because the true psychopath has no feelings of remorse, and is devoid of conscience. He is thus able to shut off his criminal activity from his normal everyday life. Intellectually he knows it is wrong to kill, but he feels that his is a special case and that it is not wrong *for him* to do so. The desire to have power over others is an essential part of the syndrome in almost all cases.

In many cases, traumatic events in childhood may trigger the development of a psychopathic personality, and if this early development can be recognized and psychiatric treatment instituted, it may be possible to save the victim. For victim he is, just as much as the woman he strangles or the child he stabs.

The offender did not land from an alien planet. He came from amongst us. As a member of our own society, we have a responsibility towards him. But we cannot attempt to treat this dreadful sickness of the mind without understanding it, any more than we can treat sickness of the body without knowledge of its cause. Neither can we take preventive measures if we do not comprehend the roots of the problem. Locking such offenders in prison is like sweeping the dust under the carpet. The only place for these men is a secure hospital where psychiatrists can study and treat them. But first the cause of their problems must be studied and understood.

I have written this book in the hope that it may make a small contribution to the greater understanding of the problem in our society. It has been said that society gets the criminals it deserves; perhaps, soon, a more understanding society will get fewer of these men who perpetrate the most horrendous deeds.

Georgina Lloyd
1986

# CHAPTER ONE

## The Red Spider of Katowice

22 July 1964 was a national holiday in Poland, commemorating the defeat of the German invaders of Warsaw by the Russians in 1944. On this twentieth anniversary a great military parade was to be staged in Warsaw.

One hundred and sixty miles north of Warsaw in the town of Olsztyn, the School of Choreography and Folklore had organized its own parade in celebration of the event. A pretty seventeen-year-old blonde, Danuta Maciejowicz, was one of many teenagers who flocked to watch the parade in Olsztyn's main thoroughfare. When she failed to return home at the expected time, the alarm was raised. Her parents and friends searched for her all along the route the parade had taken and called at the homes of her high school classmates in case she had visited one of them, but without result. Fearing for her safety, her parents notified the Police of her disappearance. It was completely out of character for Danuta, who had no boy friends and was of a quiet and studious disposition, to fail to return home at the expected time. She, like the rest of her family, was a devout Catholic. She was happy at home and devoted to her parents, brothers and sisters; it was unthinkable that she could have run away.

The next morning it became all too apparent what fate had befallen Danuta Maciejowicz. A gardener coming on duty at 7 a.m. in the Park of Polish National Heroes in Olsztyn discovered her naked body in the shrubbery. She had been raped and the lower parts of her body horribly mutilated.

The following day, 24 July, the editor of *Kulisy*, a Warsaw newspaper, received a letter written in red ink in a spidery hand. It read:

> 'I plucked a rose in bloom in the gardens of Olsztyn, and I shall do it again elsewhere, for there is no holiday without a funeral.'

The letter was unsigned.

When the letter was handed to the Warsaw Police they immediately called to mind an incident which had occurred about three weeks earlier. On 4 July, Marian Starzyński, the editor of *Przegląd Polityczny*, another Warsaw newspaper, had received an anonymous letter in spidery red handwriting which read:

> 'There is no happiness without tears, no life without death. Beware! I shall give you cause for weeping.'

Marian Starzyński had thought that the writer bore him some personal grudge, and had requested Police protection. The Police were more inclined to think it the work of a crank, possibly someone who disagreed with the newspaper's political views. In a Communist country such a person would, after all, be unlikely to come out into the open with anti-government opinions, for fear of reprisals. The Police did not think there was a serious threat to the editor's life. So they paid him one or two token reassuring visits, filed his complaint with the letter, and forgot about it.

Until now.

On comparing the letter Starzyński had received with the one sent to the editor of *Kulisy*, it was immediately apparent to the Police that the writer of both missives was one and the same person. So their anonymous letter-writer was a rapist-murderer as well as a crank. The Olsztyn Police stepped up their hunt for the slayer of Danuta Maciejowicz, while in Warsaw the Police were more vigilant than usual . . .

Their vigilance was unavailing. On 16 January 1965 yet another Warsaw newspaper, *Zycie Warszawy*, published the photo of a pretty sixteen-year-old high-school cheer-leader, Anna Kaliniak, who had been chosen to lead a parade of students in another celebration procession the next day. Anna left her home in Praga, a suburb of Warsaw, and took the ferry across the Vistula to reach the parade. Afterwards she thumbed a lift from a lorry driver who dropped her at a crossroads quite close to her home. She was not seen alive again.

The search for the missing girl was still in progress when the Police received a letter in the by now familiar red spidery hand. It told them to search a factory building opposite Anna's home, adding that, 'not all will rejoice on Poland's national days of rejoicing'. The Police switched their attention to a leather tanning works which stood opposite the young girl's home and her body was found in the basement. She had been strangled with a wire noose which the *post-mortem* showed had been dropped over her head from behind. All her clothes had been torn from her body and she had been viciously raped. After death her killer had mutilated the lower half of her body and left a six-inch metal spike thrust into her vagina.

Up to now, at any rate, it seemed that the Red Spider, as the murderer came to be known, appeared to have a compulsion to commit his crimes on national holidays, and that, unlike Jack the Ripper or the Boston Strangler, he did not confine his crimes to one comparatively small area but ranged far and wide. Olsztyn and Warsaw are 160 miles apart. But, like Jack the Ripper, the Red Spider had a strong dramatic sense, revealed in his sending of letters about his crimes to the police, sometimes before and sometimes after he had committed them. It was clear that his murder of Anna Kaliniak had been carefully planned, because he had been lurking in the shadows close to his victim's home, and he had removed a grating leading to the basement in the factory to gain entry. It is more than likely that he had seen

13

Anna's picture in the newspaper and obtained her address from the article accompanying it.

The first day of November was All Saints' Day. Poznań, 200 miles from Warsaw, was the home of an eighteen-year-old blonde hotel receptionist, named Janina Popielska. She was intending to go to a neighbouring village to meet a boy friend. Finding that the bus had already gone she decided to walk to the village, a distance of some three and a half miles. Somewhere along the way she met her killer, who suffocated her by holding a chloroform-soaked pad over her nose and mouth. He then ripped off her clothes and dragged her behind a packing shed where he raped her three times. After this he stabbed her to death with a screwdriver and mutilated the lower half of her body in such a revolting manner that the Police suppressed most of the details. Newspaper reports stated only that she had been raped, stabbed and mutilated after death. The Red Spider then stuffed Janina's brutalized body into a packing-case, where it was found later the same day. The Police searched the area intensively, swooping on all trains and buses leaving Poznań and questioning drivers, conductors and passengers in the hope of locating a man with bloodstained clothing, but to no avail.

The following day the editor of the Poznań newspaper *Kurier Zachodni* received one of the red-ink letters which were by now the notorious trademark of the Red Spider. It contained a quotation from the poet Stefan Zeromski's national epic *Popioły* written in 1928:

> 'Only tears of sorrow
> can wash out the stain of shame;
> only pangs of anguish
> can blot out the fires of lust.'

The police found it significant that the girl's surname, Popielska, was a derivative of the word *Popioły*, which means 'ashes'. Yes, this was a killer who planned his crimes carefully . . .

May Day, 1966, was an International Labour Day holiday. Celebrations were taking place all over Poland. A high-school student, Marysia Gałązka, seventeen years old, went out into the back garden to look for her cat in the quiet residential suburb of Zoliborz in Warsaw. When half an hour had passed and she had not returned her father went out to look for her. He did not have to go very far. In the back garden tool-shed he found her naked body, lying with her knees bent and her thighs apart in the classic rape position. But his daughter's rape was not the only horror her father found. Her killer had disembowelled her and arranged her intestines in a grotesque pattern over her thighs.

Major Stanislaw Ciszek, chief of the Warsaw Police Force's homicide squad, took over the investigation of this latest outrage personally. It was too soon for the familiar letter from the Red Spider to have arrived, but Ciszek was convinced in his own mind that this horror was yet one more example of the Red Spider's crazed compulsive killings. For, once again, the murder had been committed on a national holiday. And, once more, only the lower half of the victim's body had been mutilated. The Red Spider differed from most other sex killers in that he was apparently uninterested in the breasts or other upper parts of his victims. Only the lower regions of his victims' bodies had received his grisly attentions.

Ciszek now concentrated on going through the national crime files for unsolved murders all over Poland to see whether there were in the records any more rape-murders with a similar *modus operandi*. He found no fewer than fourteen murders, the first having taken place in April 1964, with similar features – similarities enough to show a definite pattern. These had taken place in Lublin, Radom, Kielce, Łódź, Białystok, Lomza, Bydgoszcz (with two victims) and Poznań and district (with six victims). Ciszek immediately called a conference of his top officers and collated the findings.

All the places in which the murders had been committed

were easily reached by railway. Ciszek stuck pins into a map of Poland and the pattern immediately became clear – the towns formed a rough circle all around Warsaw, but they extended much further south than north. It rather looked as though the killer had committed murders in Białystok, Lomza and Olsztyn, all north of Warsaw, only as a token gesture of extending his main territory. It seemed reasonable to suppose that he actually lived somewhere south of Warsaw and at the centre of a network of railway lines.

But where?

On Christmas Eve, 1966, three soldiers boarded a late-night train in Kraków to go to their homes in Warsaw to celebrate a traditional Polish Christmas. They were only just in time to jump on to the train as it pulled out of the station. Moving along the corridor to look for a compartment, one of them happened to cast a glance into the window of a reserved compartment.

'My God!' His voice was a choked cry. The other two men looked where he was pointing. A young girl, wearing only a leather mini-skirt lay on the floor of the compartment. Not only was the skirt slashed to ribbons but the body from the waist down was similarly slashed. It was obvious that she had been raped and that she was also dead.

Stifling back their nausea, the three servicemen ran for the guard who sent a message to the terminus at Warsaw. The driver was instructed to go straight through to Warsaw non-stop to prevent the killer from escaping at one of the intervening stations. It might cause quite a lot of inconvenience to the passengers but the killer had to be caught. Police were out in force at the terminus checking and double-checking all the passengers for anyone or anything suspicious, such as a person with bloodstained clothes, or carrying a bloody package. No one and nothing suspicious was found until the police, on checking the mail van, discovered the Red Spider's latest letter, dropped on top of the pile of mailbags. It was addressed once more to the editor of *Zycie Warszawy*, who had received a letter from the crazed killer almost two years previously, during the search for the missing Anna Kaliniak. This time the letter was brief and to the point and devoid of quotations from the classics. It merely stated, in the usual spidery red hand, 'I have done it again'. It would seem that the killer had boarded the train at Kraków, killed the girl and left the letter in the mail van on his way out again before the train had left the platform to start its journey towards Warsaw. He was becoming more and more audacious in his game of cat and mouse with the Police.

The girl was quickly identified as seventeen-year-old Janina Kozielska of Kraków. Ciszek recalled that another girl named Kozielska had been murdered in Warsaw in 1964; this proved to be Janina's sister, Aniela, aged fourteen. The Police chief knew there must be some connection and more urgently than ever the killer had to be caught.

Ciszek questioned the dead girls' family. They had no idea who could have killed their daughters, but they mentioned that the elder girl, Janina, sometimes worked as a part-time model at an academy of painting and sculpture called the Artlovers' Club in Kraków, and that her younger sister Aniela had also been a member of the club to which she went after school hours for lessons in abstract painting. Aniela had been murdered in Warsaw where she had gone on a trip to see her grandmother.

Back in his office at Police headquarters Ciszek turned over in his mind all the possibilities. He called for the reports on the two sisters to compare notes and he sent for the laboratory reports on the letters received from the Red Spider. Analyses of these gave him his first solid lead. The reports stated that the ink used to pen all the letters had been found, on chemical analysis, to be a home-made solution of artist's red paint dissolved in turpentine and water.

Ciszek turned his attention to the Artlovers' Club. The academy had 118 members from all walks of life – doctors, dentists, government officials, newspapermen, businessmen, students, housewives, even policemen. Ciszek interviewed each and every one of the members, paying special attention to any whose profession involved them in extensive railway travel.

One member, a twenty-six-year old translator who worked for the official Government publishing house, was a native of Katowice whose work caused him to travel a great deal. His name was Lucian Staniak and he was the possessor of an *ulgowy bilet*, which is a train ticket enabling the holder to travel anywhere in Poland.

Ciszek asked the club's manager to allow him to inspect Staniak's locker. Knowing that it was pointless to refuse, the manager granted him permission, since the Police chief could get a warrant for the purpose at any time. The locker was full of knives. The manager explained that many painters used knives in painting. Staniak, he said, liked to daub oil paint on canvas with a knife blade. He also supplied gratuitously the information that Staniak had a preoccupation with red paint and he showed him one of his paintings called 'The Circle of Life' hanging in one of their current exhibitions which depicted a flower being eaten by a cow, the cow being devoured by a wolf, the wolf being shot by a hunter, the hunter being killed by a car driven by a woman, and the woman lying in a field with her abdomen ripped open and flowers sprouting from her body.

Ciszek was now sure of his man. He obtained Staniak's address at 117 Aleja Wyzwolenia and telephoned the Police at Katowice, who went to the address but found no one at home. In fact Lucian Staniak was out committing another murder – his last. And '*wyzwolenie*' – freedom – was fast running out for the Red Spider of Katowice.

It was just a month after the train murder – 31 January 1967. He took pretty eighteen-year-old Bożena Raczkiewicz, a student at the Institute of Cinematographic Arts in Łódź, to a shelter at the railway station provided for the use of stranded overnight travellers. After stunning her with a vodka bottle, he cut off her clothing with a knife, raped her twice and mutilated her body with the broken bottle, on the neck of which he left clear fingerprints. All this took

18

place between 6.00 p.m. and 6.25 p.m. Then he left her there and made his getaway. Her body was found quite soon afterwards by some children, who ran all the way home screaming 'Murder! murder!' Long before they reached home, some men had searched the area where the running children's fingers had pointed, and called the Police.

Staniak was picked up at dawn the next day, before he had had an opportunity to write his usual missive to the Police or to the editor of a newspaper in Łódź. He had spent the night drinking. He realized that he had no chance of escape and after being brought to the Police headquarters at Katowice he confessed fully to twenty rape-murders. He was charged with the six murders described here as well as the other fourteen remaining on file, and for these he was sentenced to death. Later he was reprieved and committed to the asylum for the criminally insane at Katowice.

Nowadays, as the Police and the editors of newspapers in Poland go about their daily business, it is good that there is no equivalent in the Polish language of the English expression 'a red-letter day'. For the ones sent by the Red Spider of Katowice are the very last thing they want to be reminded of . . .

## CHAPTER TWO

### The Boy with a Grudge

No one who knew Howard Unruh as a quiet, withdrawn, reserved boy who shunned his boisterous schoolfellows and their noisy games and who preferred to sit quietly reading his Bible, could ever possibly have imagined him at the age of twenty-eight going berserk one September afternoon and shooting thirteen of his neighbours dead in a twelve-minute massacre, and then calmly giving himself up to the Police.

Howard Unruh was born in 1921 in Camden, New Jersey, the only child of religious, hard-working parents. The only odd thing about his uneventful boyhood was that he seemed to avoid the company of his peers. These days he would have been called a loner, but not thought to be all that odd – plenty of boys are solitary by nature. Not all conform to the gregarious, adventure-seeking stereotype of the average schoolboy.

Howard graduated from high school and planned on going to college to study pharmacy, but World War Two changed all that. He was called up and, not unwillingly, enlisted in the Army. There Howard found that the life of a soldier was much to his liking, and there he was introduced to weapons, which became a total obsession. Early in his training he became a sharpshooter. Fellow GIs often commented on the way he used to sit quietly on his bunk lovingly handling his rifle, taking it apart, cleaning it and reassembling it, over and over again. 'That guy sure has a thing about his rifle', they would say. Guns – any kind of guns – fascinated him.

The young recruit never went out with the other GIs drinking in bars or looking for girls. He would stay in barracks reading his Bible or cleaning his rifle. He even offered to clean the rifles of the other men. Finally he was drafted out to the Italian Campaign as a tank gunner in an armoured division, and distinguished himself in combat. After Italy he was sent to France, where he fought with distinction in the Battle of the Bulge.

One day a fellow-soldier felt unable to resist looking into Howard's private diary, which he knew Howard kept on a day-to-day basis. The soldier was so shocked at what he read that he heartily wished he had never given way to the temptation. Unruh had listed all the Germans he had personally killed with his machine-gun, including the date, time and place, and even how their bodies looked in death.

When the war ended Unruh was given an honourable discharge and several commendations for bravery under fire. On his demobilization his only immediate plan was to become a pharmacist. He took some high school refresher courses and then entered Temple University in Philadelphia. He also enrolled in a Bible study class, where he met a girl fellow-student and began dating her but it was just a mild flirtation that led nowhere. The only real love of his life was guns. He acquired a number of weapons and set up targets in the basement of his home, where he practised daily. His marksmanship was first class. At this time he became more and more withdrawn, and was practically a recluse. He also began to show signs of paranoia, imagining slights and insults even from people he had known all his life. His mind was consumed by the imagination of great wrongs done to him.

Just as he had kept a death list of Germans during his Army service, now Howard Unruh commenced to keep another diary, this time of petty grievances against his neighbours. His next-door neighbours, the Cohen family, seemed to be the chief target of his spite. For example, one day Mrs Cohen remonstrated with him about taking a short

21

cut through their back garden. Although he said nothing to her, he wrote the incident in his diary, adding the cryptic 'Ret. W.T.S.' – which meant 'Retaliate when time suitable'. Next was an entry noting that the Cohens had purchased a bugle as a gift for their twelve-year-old son and the noise annoyed him. Against this entry he wrote 'D.N.D.R.' – 'Do not delay retaliation'.

The word 'retaliation' seemed to have a fascination for him – it occurred no fewer than 180 times in his diary. The young man seemed to have a grudge against everybody, but it was all in his mind. No one had done him any harm, or borne him any ill-will. Even the girl he had dated had not jilted him – he had given up seeing her because it took up too much time from his gun collection and target practice. The psychiatrists who later examined him stated that they were at a loss to account for what triggered his mental condition; all they could say was that he was in a state of acute paranoia.

Howard Unruh tried to seal himself off from what he imagined to be a hostile world by building a high wooden fence around the back garden of his home, which was overlooked by his first floor rear-facing room. Even his father helped him to build it, thinking that perhaps this might help to settle his obviously disturbed mind. Its completion was to Howard a great triumph. He had succeeded in blocking out the world he hated.

His parents were never allowed to enter his room, which he kept locked at all times. They would have been more than shocked had they known of the veritable arsenal that was in their house. Howard had a 9mm Luger pistol with several clips, a number of other pistols, several thousand rounds of ammunition, a razor-sharp machete honed to a fine edge, and a hunting knife with a 9-inch blade.

One day Howard came home at 3 a.m. It was 5 September 1949. As he approached his home he observed a large gaping space in his defence against the outside world. Some practical jokers in the neighbourhood had stolen the gate to his high fence. Howard said nothing, but assumed that one of his neighbours was responsible, but could not be sure which. His hatred burned in him like white heat as he climbed the stairs to his room. As he lay, fully clothed, on his bed staring up at the ceiling, he decided that since he did not know which of his neighbours had taken the gate, he would kill them all. And that, he reasoned, would also take care of all the other slights and insults which, he imagined, they had hurled at him for the past four or five years.

At 8 a.m. Howard went downstairs for breakfast. His mother had prepared cereal and eggs for him. He sat down but did not eat. Instead, he stared at his mother without speaking, a wild look in his eyes. She sensed his intense hatred and desperation, for earlier that morning she had seen that the gate was gone. Suddenly Howard shot back his chair and rushed from the room, his eyes ablaze with uncontrolled anger. His mother was terrified and rushed to a neighbour's house. Howard was by now in his own room where he loaded the Luger and one of his other pistols which he thrust into his right-hand jacket pocket. Into the other pocket he crammed as many spare clips as he could, plus a knife. He was ready to carry out his neighbourhood execution.

Howard went downstairs and out through the back door, through the garden and into the street. His first stop was at the little cobbler's shop belonging to John Pilarczyk, a few doors from his own home. John Pilarczyk was busy repairing children's shoes for the coming school term. He had just completed the last of his mortgage payments for his shop, and was feeling particularly pleased with himself on this account. He looked up from his work as a shadow fell across the open doorway to see the tall figure of twenty-eight-year-old Unruh standing on the threshold, the limpid September sunlight filtering past him. It was his last mortal vision.

Without uttering a word, Unruh pointed the Luger at the cobbler and squeezed the trigger. The cobbler fell to the floor, killed instantly by a shot through the head. Unruh turned quickly and walked out. He made no move to replace the gun in his pocket.

23

Next door to the cobbler was the barber shop owned by Clark Hoover, a man who had known Howard since he was a little boy – as had Pilarczyk. Hoover blinked in astonishment as he spotted the deadly Luger in his neighbour's hand. He tried to shield with his own body the little boy perched in his barber's chair, six-year-old Orris Smith. The child's mother, Mrs Edwina Smith and her eleven-year-old daughter Norma stood by, petrified with fear. Unruh took his deadly aim and shot the small boy through the head. His face expressionless, he then shot the barber in the head and body. Ignoring the screams of Mrs Smith, Unruh walked calmly out into the sunlight.

He now hastened his steps slightly as he turned the corner and entered the drugstore owned by the man he hated most of all, his next-door neighbour Abe Cohen. But before Unruh could carry out his deadly purpose his path was blocked by James Hutton, an insurance agent who had known Howard for many years. In fact he was the Unruh family's own insurance agent.

'Hello, Howard,' he said, trying not to look at the Luger in his neighbour's right hand. He hoped his fear did not show in his voice, which he tried to keep as calm as possible in an effort to distract Howard.

Unruh had nothing against Hutton, but he had got in the way of what he wanted to do. Unruh fired twice, killing the unfortunate insurance agent instantly. Cohen rushed up the stairs to the stock warehouse above the store where his wife and son were checking some deliveries against the invoices. Howard ascended the stairs, inserting a fresh clip into the Luger as he did so. The stockroom door was open and Unruh was just in time to see Mrs Cohen hide in one cupboard and her son in another, but of Abe Cohen there was no sign. Unruh fired into the door of the cupboard and heard his victim fall down. As she did so her inert body pushed the door of the cupboard open and fell forward, sprawling on the carpet. She was still moaning. Unruh fired another shot into her head. He ignored the boy in the other cupboard.

Unruh's frustration was mounting to fever pitch. He had still not found Abe Cohen. Just then he heard a sound from an adjoining office and on moving into it found Abe Cohen's elderly mother, Mrs Leah Cohen, trying to telephone for the Police. He shot her twice and the telephone dropped from her hand, crashing on to the desk with a loud thud. Then, hearing a scraping sound, he looked up and saw Abe Cohen trying to escape by crawling across the roof, which he had reached by climbing out of the open window. Unruh took careful aim and shot him twice in the back. His victim rolled down the sloping roof and crashed down on to the pavement below. Unruh fired again into his head to make sure. He had been his main target . . .

Unruh now went calmly down the stairs and out into the street. As he did so he looked up to see the Cohen boy out on the roof, screaming hysterically. Unruh ignored him. He had no quarrel with the boy.

On the pavement in front of the drugstore lay James Hutton, beyond all human aid. Alvin Day, a passing motorist, whom Howard did not know, had stopped his car and was bending over the insurance agent's body to see whether he was still alive. This Good Samaritan's act was his last. Unruh calmly shot him through the head at point-blank range. Then he reloaded and calmly proceeded across the street at a leisurely pace, making no attempt to flee, or even to increase his walking speed. He noticed a car stationary at the traffic lights waiting for them to change.

Unruh walked over to the car and leaned in at the open window. The horror-struck woman driver, a Mrs Madeline Pearce, found herself staring straight into the barrel of a loaded Luger pistol. Unruh fired once, killing her instantly. Then, seeing the woman's ten-year-old son and her elderly mother sitting in the back of the car, he shot them both dead. He had never seen any of these three victims before.

Unruh now recrossed the street. He noticed a lorry driver climbing out of his cab in the next block. He fired one round – a long shot – dropping him with just a wound in the leg. He got off lightly.

Shopkeepers and restaurant owners were by now all barricading themselves behind locked doors. Unruh tried to lob a few shots through the doors of a supermarket, but the lock held. Next door was a tailor's establishment owned by Tom Fegrino, an Italian immigrant. He was away at the time, but his wife was hiding in the kitchen at the rear of the shop. 'Oh, my God!' she implored as she dropped to her knees. 'Don't shoot!' she begged, 'I've never done you any harm.'

Unruh had a ready answer – two shots from the Luger.

By now no one was left on the streets – everyone in the neighbourhood had taken refuge from the madman. But when Unruh walked outside again from Fegrino's shop he spotted a three-year-old boy, Tommy Hamilton, watching from a nearby window. Unruh's maniacal stare met the bewildered stare of the boy. He fired once, the bullet smashing the glass and killing the child instantly.

Something in Howard's clouded mind now impelled him to turn his steps towards his home. Along the way he saw a house with the front door slightly ajar. He entered the the house and found a woman and her two sons cowering in the kitchen at the rear. Obviously they had rushed to the back of the house in terror, forgetting to lock the door in their haste. Mrs Madeline Harris and her younger son were struck dumb with terror, but her elder son was made of sterner stuff and hurled himself at the deadly gunman, who fired two shots. One wounded the boy in the leg, the other wounded his mother in the shoulder. The younger boy was unharmed. Unruh left the house and made for his home, increasing his walking pace. In the distance Police car sirens could be heard. Soon the killer was back in his own home. Not long afterwards tear-gas canisters were being hurled through the windows.

Howard Unruh looked at the weapons in his hands, then laid them down with a shrug. His face was an impassive mask as he came out with his hands above his head. Fifty guns were trained on him by Police marksmen as he surrendered.

Howard Unruh never faced trail. He was committed to the New Jersey State Mental Hospital, where he has been for the last thirty years. No fewer than twenty psychiatrists have pronounced him to be incurably insane. One does not need to be a psychiatrist to agree with them.

One of them, while studying his case several years after the killings, asked him whether he was sorry for the mass murder he had committed. 'I'd have killed a thousand if I'd had bullets enough,' was his reply.

# CHAPTER THREE

## The Madman of Nebraska

Unlike Howard Unruh, there was always something a little odd about Charles Starkweather, even as a small boy. Like most other American youngsters he loved comics, football and cars, but he also liked and did many strange things. He would play practical jokes on his family which went beyond ordinary childish games. He was frequently reprimanded in school for indulging in horseplay which overstepped the mark and became violent attacks on his schoolfellows, often without provocation. He would steal milk from doorsteps and newspapers and mail from mailboxes in the neighbourhood. He had a particular liking for cutting circular, square or oblong pieces out of his clothes. When his parents remonstrated with him for spoiling perfectly good garments he retaliated by pouring coffee into the baby's pram or putting broken glass into his father's beer.

Charles Starkweather was born in 1940 in Lincoln, Nebraska, the middle one of seven children. By the time he was legally old enough to leave school – his poor academic qualifications having precluded him from any higher education – he took a job as a garbage collector. Even in this humble occupation he showed peculiarities which were commented upon by his fellow-garbagemen. He would frequently bring his truck to a grinding halt, sit behind the wheel and shout obscenities at passers-by. For this he was given a warning by the Police, and when asked why he did it he replied, 'The more I look at people the more I hate everybody. I even hate myself.'

At nineteen, Charles became infatuated with the James Dean image. He wore his hair long and delighted in wearing outrageous clothes. As he was of small stature – he was only five feet two inches – he wore built-up cowboy boots several sizes too large for him, stuffed with newspaper, to boost his height.

At this age, too, he acquired his first girl friend. She was diminutive Carol Ann Fugate, only fourteen years old but looking older with her well-developed bosom, sexy low-cut dresses and the way she had of swinging her hips. She, like Charles, was a teenage rebel. One of her favourite sayings was to tell her stepfather to go to hell. But, in her own way, she loved this strange, restless, red-haired boy – 'Little Red,' as he was called by his friends.

Charles also acquired a hunting rifle, which he was legally allowed to use – for hunting. Unfortunately this was not the true reason why he had purchased it. He thought it would be a good idea to take it with him on a robbery in order to frighten the people he was going to rob.

With this in mind, on 1 December 1957, Charles drove his beat-up old car into a gas service station and robbed the attendant, Robert Colvert, at gunpoint. He then drove the twenty-one-year-old attendant out to the open plains beyond Lincoln and shot him through the head. Robbery alone, apparently, had not been exciting enough.

Two months later he was at Carol Ann's home, waiting for her to come home from school. Mrs Bartlett, Carol Ann's mother (who had divorced and remarried) did not like this sullen young man who used to hang around her daughter. Still less did she like the way he handled a rifle which he always seemed to carry about with him these days. It was a slide-action .22 – quite a heavy weapon to be constantly carrying around. As he was fondling the rifle, Mrs Bartlett was understandably annoyed. 'Put that goddamn thing away,' she said, 'I'm fed up seeing it – and seeing you here, for that matter.'

Charles's reaction was to raise the rifle and shoot Mrs

Bartlett through the head. Hearing the shot, her husband rushed into the room. He, too, was shot dead. Just at that instant, Carol Ann arrived home.

Carol Ann looked down at the dead bodies of her mother and stepfather sprawled on the carpet. Then she looked questioningly at Charles, who stood impassively, the rifle held in both hands.

'They were gettin' in my way,' he explained calmly. 'They were tryin' to stop us bein' together.' He then stepped over the bodies and walked into Carol Ann's little sister's room. Betty Jean was a two-year-old toddler, but that did not stop Charles Starkweather from choking her to death by pushing his rifle down her throat.

Incredibly, this evil girl who made no secret of the fact that she hated her whole family and her stepfather in particular, went into the kitchen to make sandwiches for Charles and herself, then switched on the TV to watch one of her favourite programmes, while the madman who was her lover set about concealing the bodies of his victims. He dragged Jack Bartlett's body out to the chicken-coop behind the house and hid it under a pile of old rags and newspapers. Mrs Bartlett's body was given similar treatment in an outhouse a few yards down the garden. The baby's body was placed in a cardboard supermarket box and hidden under the washhouse copper. Then Charles joined Carol Ann on the sofa in front of the television and ate sandwiches and drank coffee as if nothing had happened.

It occurred to Carol Ann that relatives might call, as they frequently did. So she told Charles to write a note to be stuck on the front door. He wrote, 'Stay A Way. Every Body is Sick with the Flu.'

Not long afterwards Mrs Bartlett's older married daughter came to visit her sister. She thought the note very odd and she pounded on the door. Carol Ann refused to admit her. Puzzled and angry, her sister returned home and told her husband that the fourteen-year-old was acting strangely. Her husband called the Police.

Two officers arrived. Carol Ann refused to open the door.

'Can't you read?' she shouted through the letter-box. 'Everybody in the house is sick with the flu. The doctor told me not to allow anybody inside.'

'He didn't mean even your own relatives, did he?' persisted one of the officers.

'I'm not letting my sister come in here with her young baby.'

Carol Ann sounded so convincing that the policemen left. They had no authority to enter the house. On the way back to their car one of them called out to Carol Ann, 'Why would your brother-in-law call us over a thing like this?'

'Ask him! I don't know what goes on in his head. He doesn't like me, for one thing – he never did. And he's always worrying himself silly over something.'

Two days later Carol Ann's grandmother called. The girl refused to allow her into the house, using the same excuse. The woman went straight to the Police.

'There's something funny going on,' she said, 'she wouldn't let her own sister into the house, and now me. She's never done anything like this before. As for the story about them all having flu, it's a load of hogwash. Her voice sounded perfectly normal to me. And I saw some guy peeping through the upstairs curtains as I was leaving.'

Two officers accompanied Carol Ann's grandmother back to the house. Ignoring the 'flu' sign, one of them kicked open the door. The house was empty. At first they thought that maybe the entire family might have gone to the doctor's surgery. Then the officers searched the entire premises and discovered the bodies.

The officers quickly learned from neighbours that shortly before their arrival Carol Ann Fugate and Charles Starkweather had been seen hurriedly loading bags and cases into the youth's old car, which had then roared off at speed down the street. The Police put out an APB (all points bulletin) to pick them up on suspicion of murder. Their suspicion escalated into certainty when a gas service station attendant in the town of Bennett, sixteen miles away, reported that a girl and a youth answering to the general description of the wanted pair had stopped for gas and to repair a flat, and that the red-haired youth had also bought a box each of .22 rifle cartridges and .410 shotgun shells.

On 29 January 1958 Starkweather's car was spotted parked outside a farmhouse belonging to one August Meyer, in a distant part of the county. Sheriff Merle Karnop, with a large contingent of officers, surrounded the house and crept up to make a dawn raid. Through a megaphone, Karnop shouted for Starkweather to surrender. 'Come out with your hands in the air!' he boomed.

There was no response. At a given signal tear-gas bombs were lobbed through the windows of the farmhouse. Then the deputies moved in, guns drawn. One of them kicked in the front door. There was no sign of Starkweather or the girl, but in the hallway lay the farmer with his head nearly torn from his body by a shotgun blast. His car was found to be missing from its garage.

'Killed for his car!' gritted Karnop through his teeth, ignoring one of his deputies who was vomiting uncontrollably at the sight of the farmer's mutilated body. 'We have to catch these turkeys, and fast!'

Not long afterwards, another farmer in the area found the bodies of Robert Jensen, seventeen, and Carol King, sixteen, shot through the head in an isolated copse close by his land. Their almost-new convertible was missing. In its place stood the abandoned car which had been stolen from August Meyer. They had exchanged Meyer's old car for a newer model. In addition, the dead youth had been robbed of his wallet, and the dead girl had been stripped naked and viciously raped, and her handbag robbed and rings wrenched from her fingers. The couple's watches were missing too.

Two hundred lawmen were immediately deployed to comb the plains around Lincoln and Bennett, but they were too late to save the life of wealthy industrialist Charles Ward. When the businessman failed to appear at his office, a relative who worked with him became suspicious. It was not like Charles to behave this way. A very considerate man, he invariably telephoned the office if he was unavoidably delayed or sick. The relative decided to call at Charles's home to find out the cause of this out-of-character silence. He looked into the garage first, and discovered that a Ford 1956 convertible had been substituted for Ward's 1958 Buick. He immediately called the Police, who, unable to make the front door budge – it was made of solid oak – smashed a window and entered the house. They found Ward sprawled in the hallway with a bullet in his head.

On a hunch, one of the officers went upstairs and looked into the bedrooms. In one of them was the mutilated body of Clara Ward, Charles's wife; in the adjoining room was the body of her maid, Lilian Fenci. Both women had been gagged, tied, raped and then stabbed to death with ferocious frenzy.

The hunt was now stepped up to include 1,200 men. Among these were 200 National Guardsmen as well as policemen and soldiers. This madman must be captured quickly before he could kill again – as most assuredly he would – and did. Luck was with Starkweather as he eluded this massive dragnet and made it over the State line into Wyoming. A little distance outside the small town of Douglas, Charles Starkweather came across a car parked just off the freeway. Shoe salesmen Merle Collison had pulled over for an afternoon snooze before continuing on his way. He had driven clear through two states that day and that was a lot of driving. He was exhausted. Nothing that a nap wouldn't put right, though.

That nap was to be his last. He was awakened by the crash of a bullet through the window of his car. It whizzed past his ear but did not graze him. He shot out of his seat. 'Hey, man!' he shouted, 'what's you-all playin' at?'

The apparition with flaming red hair and wild eyes advanced towards him, brandishing a loaded .22. 'I ain't playin', mister,' he said, 'this is for real. Now get outa that car.'

Petrified with fear, Collison obeyed. As he did so Starkweather shot him nine times. 'Hey, Carol Ann!' he called to the girl who stood a little way behind him, 'we just got ourselves a new car!'

'What d'ya want a new car for?' queried the girl, 'you just gotta new Buick. This one ain't so good.'

'That ain't the point, honey,' was the reply, 'the po-leece are lookin' for us in a Buick. This one's a Chrysler. The po-leece ain't figurin' on lookin' for us in a Chrysler when we're on our way.'

The new car, however, was proving bothersome. The emergency brake was jammed. Try as he might, Charles could not get it free. He was still struggling frantically with it when Carol Ann shouted to him that a police car was approaching them round a bend in the road.

As Deputy Sheriff William Rohmer drove up and skidded to a stop with a screech of tyres, Starkweather dropped his rifle, jumped over the dead body of Collison and raced for the Buick. Carol Ann, screaming hysterically, ran towards the lawman. 'Help, help!' she screamed, 'the guy's crazy!'

The deputy thrust the girl into the back of his car and took off after the speeding Buick, radioing to his headquarters for backup. Another police car was soon joining in the chase, which reached 115 miles an hour. A well-aimed shot blew a hole in one of the Buick's tyres and the car went spinning out of control on to the grass verge. It came to a sudden stop in the hedge. Starkweather emerged, shouting and swearing at the officers who converged round him and covered him with drawn guns.

In court, the killer at first tried to protect his girl friend, saying that he had taken her as a hostage and that she had taken no part in the killings and robberies. Later, however, when Carol Ann protested her innocence, branding her lover as a murderer and robber, he turned on her.

'She could have escaped and left me any time she wanted to,' he said. 'I left her alone lots of times. Sometimes when I would go into some joint to fetch us hamburgers and French fries, or Cokes, I'd leave her there alone sitting in the car with all them guns. There would-a been nothin' to stop her from running away. Once she even said that the

34

hamburgers were lousy an' that we should go back in there and shoot all them folks in the restaurant. Then there was that time I shot her folks and killed her baby sister. She never said nothin'. All she did while I was gettin' rid of the bodies was to sit an' watch television an' make us some food an' coffee in the kitchen. She sure wasn't no hostage. I jus' made that up.'

The jury ignored the girl's plea of not guilty. Carol Ann Fugate was given a sentence of life imprisonment. Starkweather received a death sentence and was lodged in death row in Nebraska State Penitentiary.

On 24 June 1959 Charles Starkweather went to the electric chair. The time was 12 midnight. At 12.03 a.m. the prison doctor, Paul Getscher, announced to the statutory witnesses who were present that Charles Starkweather was dead. At nineteen, he was one of the youngest murderers ever to die in the electric chair.

Outside the gates of the prison thirty teenage girls, in blue jeans and bobby-sox, milled around a newspaper reporter. One of them, acting as their spokesman, stepped forward towards the reporter.

'Some of us knew Charles,' she said, 'some of us just wanted to be with him at the end . . .'

# CHAPTER FOUR

## The Clue of the Whodunnit

'Officer! officer!'

The patrolling policeman, plodding along on his beat in one of Berlin's working-class suburbs, stopped in his tracks and turned in the direction of the voice which had hailed him. Across the street he saw a workman in cloth cap and work-stained overalls waving his arm to attract his attention.

'What's the matter, chum?' The policeman was a friendly sort of chap and always willing to help anyone.

'I can't get into my flat!' said the greatly-agitated workman, who was still waving his arm as he drew level with the officer.

'Forgotten your key?'

'Oh, no, officer!' said the man, fumbling in his pockets and eventually producing a small bunch of keys, 'it's not that. I've been trying to get into my flat these last fifteen minutes. The door is bolted on the inside. Something must be wrong. My wife never bolts the door in the daytime, what with me coming in from work and the kids going in and out. We only lock up at night before we go to bed.'

'Have you tried knocking very loudly? Perhaps your wife's asleep, or in the bath,' suggested the policeman.

'Look!' replied the man, 'I've hammered on the door and called her name, but there's no reply. Can't even hear any of the kids, either. Something must be wrong, officer! I need some help to get into my flat!'

The policeman took out his notebook. 'What's your name?'

'Konrad Beck.'

'Well, Mr Beck, we'll go and take a look at your flat and see whether we can find out why you can't get into it. Perhaps you will lead the way . . .'

The flat was just around the corner in a working-class tenement block. The two men trudged up to the second floor and came to a halt in front of No.24. The policeman rapped sharply on the door. 'Police! Open up!' he called loudly. Again he repeated his knock, more loudly this time. 'Open up! Police!'

There was no reply.

The workman took off his cap and brushed his hair back from his brow in a nervous gesture, and replaced his cap. 'I can't understand it,' he said, 'the children should be there. I've got five of them. The youngest is only four. The others go to school, but there's no school today being Saturday. Can you break in? Something *must* be wrong.'

'You seem to be pretty sure that something's wrong,' observed the officer, 'maybe they've all gone out to the cinema or something.'

'My wife wouldn't be able to afford to go to the cinema with all the children,' said Beck, 'anyway, she's always in at this time getting the supper ready.'

'I'm not authorized to break into your flat,' said the policeman. 'Tell me where I can find the landlord, and we'll ask him if he can get in. I expect he has a master key for emergencies.' Konrad Beck gave him the number of the flat in the next block where the landlord lived with his family. 'Wait here till I get back,' the officer told him. Then he went off to find the landlord.

Although the landlord was in, unfortunately he did not keep any spare keys, but as it appeared to be an emergency he gave the policeman permission to use force to effect an entry. He was unable to do so – the door would not budge.

'The only thing to do will be to get a carpenter to take the door off its hinges,' he said. 'It seems that there is a bolt keeping the door firmly in position.'

After some neighbourhood inquiries a carpenter and his

mate were found who proceeded to lever the door from its jamb so that the hinges could be removed. The removal of the hinges still left the door in such a position that it would have to be forced, and the reason for this was discovered as the workmen, the policeman and Konrad Beck squeezed their way into the flat past the tilted door, kept in position by the bolt. The bolt had been kept well oiled so that it moved smoothly and easily, and it had been pushed all the length of its metal groove.

Entering the living-room which opened off the hallway, the four men gasped in horror at the sight which met their gaze. Hanging by a rope from a hook in the room, normally used for hats and coats, was Frau Renate Beck. Her clothes were threadbare, and the shoes which had dropped from her dangling feet were run down, with holes in the soles. The nails on her fingers were broken from rough work. Her grey hair was uncared-for and scraped up into a bun, and the face above the strangling noose was blue with cyanosis. From her mouth the tongue protruded grotesquely.

'Is this your wife?'

The question seemed to rouse Konrad Beck from the stupor into which shock had thrown him.

'Yes.' His legs tottered under him as he made for the nearest chair, where he sat down heavily without speaking, his head in his hands.

'Where are the children?'

Beck shook his head dazedly. 'I don't know,' he replied.

The policeman looked round the flat briefly. 'They don't seem to be here,' he said. Then, almost out of idle curiosity, he opened the door of a large cupboard in the hall. The door was fastened only by a simple drop-latch. As he opened the door the policeman gasped aloud, 'Mein Gott!' The carpenters came up behind him to find out what he had seen, and Beck roused himself from his chair and joined them. The sight that confronted them was even more ghastly than the one in the living-room.

Hanging from the cupboard hooks, just as though they were garments, were five small bodies, blue-faced in death.

Suspended by ropes, the five children of Konrad Beck ranged in age from little Renate, four, to Heinz, twelve. All the children were dressed in old clothes that were little more than rags. Three of them wore no shoes or socks. All of them were thin and undernourished.

The men cut down all the hanging bodies and police reinforcements were summoned together with the police doctor, Heinrich Grünwald, who pronounced that the woman had strangled all the children by hanging and then hanged herself. 'She must have come to the end of her endurance,' he said. 'Five mouths to feed and not enough to eat or clothe themselves. Funny thing, though – Herr Beck doesn't look undernourished to me. Quite a healthy specimen from what I can see. And I understand he's working, you say – so he must be earning. What is his trade?'

One of the carpenters, who knew Beck, supplied the doctor with the answer to his question. 'He's a totter. Drives a horse and cart and moves furniture, clears old houses, sells unwanted furniture, that kind of thing.'

Konrad Beck was conscious of many eyes watching him, observing his reactions. Two of the police officers asked him a number of questions. Had he quarrelled with his wife? He shook his head and pointed out that a carter's wages were low and there were seven of them to feed and clothe, after paying the rent and other household expenses. Was his wife other than her normal self lately? Had anything been worrying her? Again Beck shook his head. Did they owe anyone money? Oh, yes, was the reply. Who, among the lower middle working classes, didn't? Shopkeepers, mostly. They were partly to blame for giving so much credit, especially when they knew that the customers had hardly two pfennigs to rub together.

Tick, on the slate, was quite common in 1881.

The Police had all the bodies removed to the local morgue, and the carpenters then set about repairing the door. Before leaving, the police officers asked Konrad Beck to call in at the police station after he had satisfied himself that his door was repaired, to make his formal statement for their records.

When Beck arrived at the police station he was shown into the office of Commissioner Heinz Hollmann, who had already perused the doctor's preliminary report and also the report made out by the policeman whom Beck had originally called to the scene. He asked Beck some further questions, wrote his answers in his notebook and then told Beck that he was free to go. But he was puzzled by a number of aspects of the case. What woman, however poor and destitute, would kill all her own children, even if she wanted to commit suicide? Even if the younger children had put up little or no resistance, it must have been quite a difficult feat for a woman as thin and frail-looking as Renate Beck to hang the older ones. Then, again, why was her husband so robust and healthy-looking and his working clothes in such good repair and condition? Hollmann's logical Teutonic thinking could not accept that everything was as it seemed in this case.

He sent for the original beat policeman who had been first on the scene and said to him, 'I want you to make some discreet inquiries in the neighbourhood about this Beck family. Find out everything you can about them – especially about Konrad Beck. But be discreet. Don't let anyone suspect that you're acting officially. Keep it all very casual.'

Two days later Hollmann received his report. It appeared that although Beck's earnings as a carter were reasonably good, he deliberately kept his wife short of money. His wife frequently had to ask neighbours for old clothes for the children and even for food. Beck was frequently away from home, sometimes for several days at a stretch, and no one seemed to know where he went. It was supposed that he had some haulage jobs outside the German capital. When he was at home, neighbours were quick to point out, he never helped his wife in the house or with the children, but always had his nose in a book. He was, apparently, an avid reader.

As far as Renate Beck herself was concerned, she had, apparently, made few friends, and had never mentioned suicide to anyone. She rarely went out, possibly because she was ashamed of her shabby clothes.

What kind of books did Beck read? No one seemed to know. But Hollmann wanted to find out. So one day he went to Beck's flat, ostensibly to inspect the repaired front door and see that the workmen had made a proper job of it. Beck asked Hollmann in for a cup of coffee. While Beck was out in the kitchen brewing the coffee the Commissioner cast his observant glance around the sitting-room. On a shelf were a number of tattered books, almost all sensational novels. No classics or anything like that. When Beck came in with the coffee Hollmann again turned his attention to the door.

Beck watched Hollmann as he experimented. He closed the door and shot the bolt, satisfying himself that there was no possible means of entering the flat with the door bolted on the inside. The windows were set well above the level of the landing, and the walls were perfectly flush, with no guttering or pipes which could afford a foothold, neither were there any ledges at window-level. He paced all the rooms of the flat. It seemed impossible that there could be any other solution than the obvious one that Renate Beck had killed her children and then herself. He went back to the door and worked the well-oiled lock through his fingers, as though handling the mechanism would start some train of thought in his mind, but it remained an annoying blank.

Next, Hollmann decided to have one of his detectives follow Beck and keep a discreet tail on him whenever he left his flat, and report to him how he spent his time, and where. When he received the detective's report he learned that Beck was seeing a young servant girl who lived in another suburb of Berlin. From discreet inquiries, it was ascertained that Beck had been spending money on this girl for some considerable time and was even paying the rent of her room. It was also found that she had been writing letters to Beck regularly at his home address.

Hollmann and this detective arranged to visit Beck's flat the next day when Beck had left to go to work. It was not disclosed how they gained entry, but with no bolt to hamper their efforts they doubtless found a way of picking the lock. The two officers searched for the letters alleged to have been received by Beck, hoping to find some clue to the tragedy, but none was found.

'Perhaps he destroys them after reading them', suggested the younger of the two officers.

'Or hides them,' replied Hollmann. 'Perhaps he keeps them between the pages of his books.' With these words, Hollmann began thumbing through the numerous novels on the bookshelf he had noticed on his first visit. No letters were found – perhaps Konrad Beck really had destroyed them – but Hollmann's keen powers of observation led him to notice that one particular book fell open naturally at a certain page whenever he picked it up, as though it had been pressed open at that place in order to be studied several times. The book was a novel by an English writer, John Radcliffe, which had been translated into German. The title was *Nena Sahib*. The title conveyed little, but the Commissioner, intrigued, began to read the pages where the book fell open naturally. To his amazement, he found himself reading about a man, believed to have committed suicide, who was found dead in a room bolted on the inside – exactly as in the case of Renate Beck and her children!

When, in the novel, the dead man was discovered, his death was accepted as suicide until an English private detective, snooping around, discovered a tiny hole that had been pierced through the woodwork of the door beside the bolt. Through this hole a strand of wire could be passed. With one end twisted into a loop and hooked over the handle of the bolt it was possible to bolt or unbolt the door on the inside by manipulating the wire from the outside. The hole had then been filled in with putty.

Hollmann did not bother to finish reading the novel. He turned to his assistant and told him to arrange for some workmen to remove the door to Beck's flat and bring it to headquarters. Two hours later the door was lying across Hollmann's desk.

Near the edge, a few centimetres from the bolt on the other side, Hollmann found a tiny excrescence. Paring this away with a sharp-bladed penknife, he had the pieces examined in the laboratory, where they were found to be composed of tinted sealing-wax. A tiny hole had been exposed in the wood at the point where the wax had been removed. A packing needle was pushed through the hole and the wax filling removed. Adhering to some of the wax particles were strands of horsehair.

Hollmann was jubilant. Konrad Beck drove a horse and cart. A tiny loop made of horsehair strands would be much safer to use for the purpose than a piece of wire. If a piece of wire had slipped from his fingers at the last moment it would have fallen to the ground on the inside of the door and provided damning evidence that would convict him. Horsehair was almost invisible compared with wire, and noiseless in use. All Beck would have to do after using a loop made of horsehair strands would be to fill the tiny hole with sealing-wax, rub it down level with the surface of the door and tint it on each side of the hole to match the paint on the door.

Before announcing that he had solved the mystery, Hollmann was thorough enough to test his theory first. He sent a policeman to procure some horsehair, from which he made a tiny thin-stranded loop. He had to experiment several times before the horsehair had the right amount of rigidity to enable him to move the bolt caught in the looped end. He knew then why the bolt had been kept so well-lubricated. Had it been in the least stiff or rusty, it would have been impossible to manipulate in this way. He also realized that the action of drawing the horsehair through the tiny hole had severed a few of the strands, because the hole was not completely smooth inside but bore a few minute splinters of wood. This is why he found several strands of horsehair caught in the scraps of wax he had removed from the hole.

He had barely arrived at his final conclusions when an angry Konrad Beck was shown into his office. 'What's the idea?' he blustered. 'Who gave you permission to take the door off my flat? Anyone can break in and steal! A burglar could just walk in from the street!'

'And take your books, maybe? Mr Beck, you don't need your door where you're going. There nobody will be able to steal anything from you. And the doors there are all made of steel, not wood.'

'What are you talking about?' bluffed Beck, now visibly agitated but trying desperately to control his voice.

'Why did you kill your wife, Mr Beck? Wouldn't a divorce have been better? And – Gott in Himmel! Why did you kill your children? Didn't your mistress want a ready-made family?'

Konrad Beck stumbled to a chair and sat down, a broken man. He knew that it was useless to deny the truth any further.

'She insisted on marriage,' muttered Beck, more to himself than to Hollmann. 'It had to be marriage, or she would not see me again. I couldn't bear to lose her. I loved her . . .'

'And for that one girl, you murdered not only your wife but all five of your children!' Words failed the Commissioner as he stared at the other man uncomprehendingly.

Hollmann beckoned to two burly constables to lead Beck to the cells, after he had first been handcuffed and read his rights. Another officer was detailed to place the door in storage until it would be required as evidence in court, together with the scraps of sealing-wax and strands of horsehair, which were placed in a sealed envelope. Then the Commissioner set to writing out his own report to complete the file on the man who would be accused of the wanton murder of his entire family.

During the trial Beck made much of the letters, which he had in fact destroyed. He stated that these amounted to blackmail, inasmuch as his mistress had threatened that unless he did something quickly to resolve his marital situation and marry her, he would never see her again. Predictably, these letters did not constitute mitigation, and the defence literally had no case on his behalf. Not only the door, the sealing-wax fragments and the horsehair strands but also the book which had inspired Beck's deadly imitation were produced in evidence at his trial. Women jurors wept as they were shown photographs of his young children. His fate was sealed.

The jury unanimously found him guilty, and he was sentenced to death. As he was led out of the court he had the face of an old man, although he was only forty. He was executed on 4 December 1881.

# CHAPTER FIVE

## The Monster of Rügen

Polish-born Jadwiga Heidemann, who lived with her German construction-worker husband Ulrich in the village of Lechtingen, near Osnabrück in the northern part of what is now West Germany, was worried. It was already 12.30 p.m. and little Hannelore, her seven-year-old daughter, had not come home from school for her mid-day meal. The village school was only 300 yards from the Heidemanns' cottage, and Hannelore was normally home well before 12.15 p.m., since morning school finished at 12.00 noon. Where could the child have got to? It was unlike her to dawdle. All the children came home from school at midday; there was no such thing as school dinners in Germany in 1898.

Just then there was a knock at the back door. Ah, here she was now! But no, it could not be – Hannelore had no need to knock. The back door was always left open for her when she was expected home from school.

Puzzled, Frau Heidemann opened the door, to find her neighbour, Frau Irmgard Langemeier, on the doorstep. She, too, had a puzzled frown.

'Jadwiga!' she cried. 'Is Else with you? Did she come home with Hannelore?'

'Hannelore hasn't come home yet,' replied Frau Heidemann, trying desperately to conceal the note of rising concern in her voice. 'Why, Irmgard – what is it? It seems the girls are *both* late for once! The teachers never keep children in at lunch-time, so there must be some other cause. Maybe they've gone to play somewhere and forgotten the time.'

'Oh, but Jadwiga, you *know* they never do that at lunch-time! Maybe after school finishes in the afternoon – but not now. Their appetites are too big for that!'

Frau Langemeier was less adept at hiding her feelings. A farm labourer's wife, she was forthright and down-to-earth by nature.

'Else would never go off somewhere and play after morning school,' she continued. 'It's twenty to one already. Something must have happened to her!'

'Perhaps she had an accident – tripped and cut herself, maybe, and Hannelore has taken her back to school for one of the teachers to give her first aid.' Frau Heidemann tried to make her voice sound convincing, but she was far from convinced herself. But she did not wish to alarm her neighbour unnecessarily. There might be some simple explanation. Being neighbours, the two girls had grown up together and had continued their friendship at school, where Else, who was barely a year older than Hannelore, was in the next class.

'I'll tell you what,' Frau Heidemann continued, 'we'll give them until one o'clock and then we'll go to the school. I'll come round for you . . .'

At the school, the two women were told that neither Hannelore nor Else had attended school at all that day and no one had seen them. By now thoroughly alarmed, they rounded up all their friends and neighbours and fetched their husbands from their work. The search party spread out and combed the entire village, looking into barns, sheds, deserted buildings – anywhere where two little blonde girls could have played hide-and-seek, got themselves accidentally locked in somewhere, or become lost. Three hours of searching produced no results, and it was decided to range farther afield and search the woods in the vicinity of the village before darkness descended on that mild evening of 9 September.

The searchers in the woods had not been looking for long before they came upon the body of Hannelore Heidemann, horribly mutilated. Parts of her body had been dismembered and strewn about in the forest. The search for Else continued, and later that same evening her pitiful remains were found in some bushes, butchered even more hideously, if that were possible, than those of the younger child.

The Police were called and lost no time in questioning everyone in the village and its vicinity, soon after the first body had been found. A villager mentioned that he had seen the local carpenter, a journeyman named Ludwig Tessnow, walking into the village from the direction of the woods earlier that day. The informant noted that the carpenter's clothing was heavily stained with dark reddish-brown blotches. The Police took Tessnow into custody, still wearing his stained clothing, and questioned him as to his movements that day. He stated that he had been working, doing various odd jobs for people in the area. Questioned about the stains on his clothes, he stated that they were his working clothes and that the stains were from the wood dye he used.

At that time the science of forensic pathology was in its infancy, and the Police had no means of testing cloth for bloodstains. Incredibly, they accepted their suspect's explanation without question. It was, they surmised, perfectly reasonable that a carpenter should have his working clothes stained with wood dye, and he appeared to account for his movements that day to their satisfaction. He showed no sign of nervousness or agitation, and he was released without further investigation.

The search for the monster who had destroyed two innocent little girls in so hideous a fashion continued unabated. Tessnow made no attempt to leave the village but continued with his work, neither did he make any attempt to burn the stained clothing, which he was seen to wear on several subsequent occasions. The suspicious villager who had alerted the Police to Tessnow visited the latter in his workshop under pretext of ordering some bookshelves, and while he was there he contrived to knock over a tin of wood dye so that it ran down his trousers. When the stains had dried he noticed that they looked identical to the stains on

Tessnow's working clothes. Perhaps, after all, he had been too hasty in his judgement. After all, if the fellow were guilty he would have left the village a long time ago . . .

Months passed and the Police were no nearer finding the 'Beast of the Woods'. They were still looking for clues in January 1899, when Tessnow left Lechtingen to go to work in another part of Germany.

On 1 July 1901 Peter, aged six, and Hermann, aged eight, the sons of a carter named Hans-Peter Stubbe, disappeared from their home on the Baltic island of Rügen. They had gone out to play, as boys do the world over, and had not come home at the usual time for their supper in their parents' modest house in the village of Göhren, in the south-eastern area of Rügen. When they had not come home by dusk, their father, with several neighbours and the village policeman, set out to look for them.

The village of Göhren adjoined an extensive tract of woodland, and Stubbe thought that his sons might have gone into the woods to play, and got lost, as the woods stretched for several miles and in the dark the children could easily confuse the many footpaths. The search party spread out with torches, calling the boys' names, but finding no clues after several hours, they gave up the hunt until dawn the next day, when the light would make searching easier. Soon after sunrise one of the neighbours of the boys' father found the remains of both bodies hidden in a thicket. The boys had been killed with a large stone, found bloodstained nearby, which had been used to crush their skulls. The children had then been decapitated, their limbs amputated and their bodies cut open. The elder boy's heart had been removed, and was never found.

Police questioned the shocked villagers at home, at work, wherever they found them. No one escaped their close scrutiny. The same day, 2 July, a fruit-seller told police that she had seen the two children talking in the late afternoon of the previous day to a journeyman carpenter named Ludwig Tessnow, who lived in a neighbouring village. This man, she said, was well-known as an eccentric. He was a native of Rügen and had only recently returned to his native island, having in the meantime been working all over Germany. The same evening a road worker reported that he had seen Tessnow, whom he knew, walking home the night before, and that his clothing was 'covered with brownish spots'.

Tessnow was immediately arrested, and his home was searched. When arrested he was wearing clean clothes which showed no signs of staining of any kind. At his home a wardrobe was searched and there the Police found several garments which gave the appearance of having been recently washed – indeed, some were still damp, including a jacket, trousers, collar and tie and a cloth cap. A waistcoat and shirt were found which bore brownish spots and stains, and a heavily-stained pair of boots was also found under the stone sink in the kitchen, as though awaiting cleaning by being washed rather than by being polished in the normal way.

Questioned intensively by the Police, Tessnow had a plausible account of his movements on 1 July and when asked about the spots and stains on his clothing he said that these were made by the wood dye he used in his work. Unlike the more gullible Police officers who had questioned him in September 1898, however, the Police at Rügen were not satisfied with Tessnow's glib answers, and he was sent for trial before the examining magistrates at Greifswald.

The examining magistrate, Johann-Klaus Schmidt, on reading the accused's statement, noticed his explanation that wood dye was the source of the stains on his clothing, and was immediately struck by the resemblance of this case to another case he had read about three years earlier, in which a suspect in a similar child-murder case had offered the very same explanation for stains found on his clothes. In that case the suspect had never been charged, and had been released owing to lack of evidence. Could that same man be the one he had now in custody? He would make inquiries as to where that case had taken place, and get in touch with the Police there.

Schmidt was also struck by certain similar features in a report that, three weeks earlier on 11 June 1901, seven sheep had been horribly butchered in a field near Göhren. Their bodies had been slit open, cut to pieces, and the viscera scattered all over the field. The owner of the sheep had been too late to catch the killer, but had seen a man running away, and claimed that he would recognize him again.

Schmidt sent a memo to the Police authorities in Osnabrück, and learned that the journeyman carpenter who had been temporarily held on suspicion of a double child murder on 9 September 1898 was Ludwig Tessnow of Baabe on the island of Rügen, and that owing to lack of evidence positively connecting him with the crime, he had been released. The crime had never been solved and remained on file as a murder by person or persons unknown.

Schmidt now had Tessnow placed in an identification parade and arranged for the owner of the sheep to be brought to the prison yard at Greifswald. He immediately picked out Tessnow without hesitation as the man he had seen running from his field after the massacre of his flock.

Tessnow, when interrogated about this outrage – which had been thought to be the work of a madman or someone involved in witchcraft rites – denied all knowledge of the incident apart from what he had read in the newspapers, and averred that he had never killed a harmless animal, much less an innocent child. He persisted in his statement that the stains on his clothes were due to wood dye.

In 1898, when Tessnow had been held on suspicion of the murders of the two little girls in Lechtingen, forensic pathology had not yet advanced to a stage where chemical tests on stains could differentiate blood from other substances. But by 1901 Paul Uhlenhuth had developed his pioneering method of testing bloodstains, and Tessnow's clothing was sent to his laboratory. The prosecutor Ernst Hübschmann at Greifswald had just heard of Uhlenhuth's work and had summoned a meeting with examining magistrate Schmidt about the Tessnow case. The test, Hübschmann told Schmidt, could prove that stains were blood or otherwise, and could also differentiate between human and animal blood.

On 29 July and 1 August 1901 Professor Uhlenhuth received two packages containing the clothing of Ludwig Tessnow, and also a bloodstained stone, alleged to have been the murder weapon in the Stubbe case. As by this time the newspapers were attacking the Police for their failure to obtain a confession from the suspect they had in their custody, and the people were openly complaining of the apparent inability of the authorities to bring the murderer to justice, Schmidt requested Uhlenhuth to conduct his tests with the utmost speed consistent with obtaining conclusive results.

Uhlenhuth, with his assistant Schumacher, examined nearly 100 separate spots and stains on Tessnow's clothing. His report, dated 5 August 1901, confirmed that human blood had incontrovertibly been demonstrated in six places on the jacket, seven places on the trousers, four on the waistcoat, one place on the shirt and one place on the cap. Sheep's blood had been demonstrated conclusively in six places on the jacket and three on the trousers. Thus was it proved that Ludwig Tessnow had not only butchered the sheep but had also committed the ghastly murders of Hermann and Peter Stubbe. The stone, too, had given up its grim secret. In addition, various identical similarities in the 1898 and 1901 cases proved that the 'Monster of Rügen' had also been responsible for the grisly murders of little Hannelore Heidemann and Else Langemeier.

The trial of Ludwig Tessnow provided an arena for the soft-spoken and still youthful Professor Uhlenhuth to establish his revolutionary new method of testing bloodstains, and of showing that his method could also differentiate between human blood and the blood of various mammals. The method was hailed as a great advance in forensic pathology and a breakthrough in medical jurisprudence. His findings were – as are all revolutionary new methods – challenged by the more orthodox practitioners of these sciences, but in the event were proved correct, and were the means of bringing many notorious criminals to justice, long before the more modern science of blood grouping and typing superseded them.

The thirty-nine-year-old carpenter, who thought he could fool the Police a second time that the stains of his victims' blood were wood dye, was executed in Greifswald Prison in 1904.

# CHAPTER SIX

## The Landladies under the Bed

Not every psychopathic criminal can point to a hereditary taint or a deprived childhood, but Earle Nelson had both. His mother, of Hispanic origin and but twenty when she gave birth to him on 12 May 1897, died ten months later from syphilis, which she had contracted from her husband. Venereal diseases in those days were less amenable to treatment with drugs than they are now, and left to run its course syphilis usually ended up carrying off the afflicted person with general paralysis of the insane. Earle Nelson's father succumbed just seven months after his wife.

After both his parents had died, the infant Earle was brought up by his aunt, Mrs Lilian Fabian. As he grew from babyhood to boyhood, the unfortunate Mrs Fabian was all too soon to discover that the child had not escaped the dreadful legacy of his parents' insanity even at this early stage. He had none of the boisterous outgoing personality which characterized most normal boys, but was sullen, morose and withdrawn, a loner who did not like to play with other boys and who stayed at home rather than go out.

When he was ten years old, Earle was hit by a tram on one of the rare occasions when he left the house, and was unconscious for five or six days. Hospital doctors diagnosed concussion, since the boy had been hit on the side of the head in this accident. After his release from hospital, he began to suffer from frequent headaches and periodic dizzy spells, which became worse as he grew older. By the time he reached puberty his headaches had become so violent that frequently he was unable to stand upright from the intensity of the pain. Mrs Fabian, a widow, had to work to keep herself, Earle and her own two children, and the long hours of her work as a seamstress were given as the reason for neglecting to take Earle to a doctor for treatment.

In his later teenage years, Earle developed a pattern of eccentric behaviour which his aunt found very hard to cope with. He would stay at home for a few days and then suddenly walk out without warning, staying away for two or three weeks and then just as suddenly come back home, walking in as though nothing had happened. Asked for an explanation, he would say he had been looking for work.

Earle would not wait for others at table but would eat when he liked. He would show off in company, walking on his hands, picking up heavy oak chairs with his teeth, and shocking guests with obscene language. He had a habit of constantly changing his clothes several times a day. If a new suit was purchased for him, he would go out and sell it for two or three dollars and come in wearing rags instead. Given new woollen underwear, he would sell that too, and return devoid of any undergarments, even in the middle of winter. He would wear cheap flashy imitation jewellery purchased at five-and-ten stores. On one occasion his aunt had purchased some new boots for him and he wore them to walk through a stream in which the water reached up to his knees.

If his aunt remonstrated at his odd behaviour he would just smile and say nothing, but later he would become abusive instead. From that point onwards, Mrs Fabian dared not say anything to annoy him. He used to leave the house late at night and wander about in the streets, and wake the whole neighbourhood by banging on the locked door to be allowed in. On one occasion in the winter, he brought a quantity of ice into the house and strewed it all over the floors of several of the rooms in the middle of the night. Mrs Fabian got to the point where she was afraid to have him sleep in the house at night, and used to give him money to sleep in an hotel. The record does not say how the hotel-keepers managed to cope with him.

It is hard to speculate whether this personality disorder stemmed from inherited tendencies, or whether the head injury from the street accident was responsible. It might well have been a combination of both. Taken together, all his symptoms pointed to an advance warning of an unstable personality, an abnormal mentality, which is often the prelude to the début of a homicidal maniac.

Earle Nelson's first recorded crime took place on 21 May 1918 when he went to a neighbour's basement to collect some tools he had been using when doing a job for the neighbour, and while there attempted to assault the man's child. She screamed, and her father rushed to the scene, fought with Nelson and overpowered him, and took him to the Police station.

In court Earle admitted the attempted assault, and when asked why he had thus incurred the wrath of a neighbour with whom he had been on good terms, he put forward the irrelevant excuse that he was 'feeling fed up at the time because he had applied to join the Navy and they had turned him down'. The judge commented that this was scarcely a reason for attempting to assault a little girl. The judge looked into the matter of Earle's U.S. Navy application and found that when examined by the naval hospital board they had found him unfit to join by reason of 'unstable personality bordering on insanity'. The red warning light – but no one seemed to think anything more was necessary than a short jail term followed by a spell in the Napa State Hospital for Mental Defectives. Even after his aunt visited him there and found him in a straitjacket tied to his bed (because he had plucked out all his eyebrows) no one seemed unduly alarmed.

As if this was not enough, he escaped three times from the mental hospital. After one of his escapes, his aunt, who had barely finished writing in a letter to a relative how much safer she felt now that her nephew was confined to what she described as the 'lunatic asylum', looked up and was terrified to see him with his face pressed to the window looking in at her 'with a terrible insane look in his eyes'. After his next and last escape he was free two and a half years, before being recaptured and reconfined under an insanity warrant signed by a California Superior Court judge. On 2 November 1923 he left the hospital, but as no one seemed to try to bring him back, perhaps 'escape' is not the right word to use on this occasion, although he certainly had not had the permission of the doctors to leave. However, he did not return to his aunt's house, and little is known of his movements until February 1926. No doubt he followed his usual pattern, bumming around, doing odd jobs, and scaring the wits out of anyone he stayed with. Perhaps he was told to leave his lodgings, which prompted him to look for new ones on 20 February 1926, in San Francisco.

Sixty-year-old Miss Clara Newman, who was a widow, lived with an orphaned semi-invalid nephew in her neat brownstone house. In straitened circumstances, she hung a sign in the ground floor front window of her home which said 'Room To Let'. Earle Nelson seemed to her to be a presentable young man, and she offered him the room. Her nephew, who was carrying an attaché-case, came down the dark and gloomy staircase as Miss Newman ascended with Nelson to show him the room, which was on the first floor, and went out. The nephew was going to stay for a few days with his brother and sister-in-law in Sacramento.

A few days later the nephew returned home, and on entering the house was at once aware of a peculiar odour which appeared to emanate from the upper portion of the house. Leaving his suitcase on the hall floor he at once went upstairs to investigate. In an attic lavatory he found the naked body of his aunt, who had been viciously raped and strangled.

The Police could do little, as there were no clues. The new lodger had, of course, long since gone, and the nephew had not seen him closely enough to be able to give any description as he had caught barely one glimpse of him on the unlit staircase. 'He was about medium height,' the nephew told Police, 'and seemed to be well-dressed.' That was all he could tell them.

Ten days later in San José, while the hue and cry for the killer was at its height in San Francisco, Mrs Laura Ernestine Beale, also sixty, was found dead in the house where she too had advertised a room to let. She had been raped and strangled in exactly the same fashion and left in a box-room among the trunks and storage cases. No one had any useful information to give the Police except a meagre description of 'a young man calling about rooms'. For some reason the local newspapers referred to him as 'the Dark Strangler', although his colouring was not particularly dark despite his half-Puerto Rican ancestry.

Nelson now doubled back to San Francisco, as though daring the Police to call his bluff, and on 10 June 1926 he called at the house of sixty-three-year-old Mrs Lilian St. Mary in response to a sign in her window which stated 'Room For Rent'. It was not long before she was found, naked, raped and strangled, pushed under a bed, by a tenant who wanted to pay his rent prior to going on holiday. Finding the door to the landlady's rooms unlocked on getting no answer to his knocks, the tenant had pushed the door open . . . Minutes later Police were going over the house, but without result. Nelson had taken care that no one had seen him, either before or after he had carried out his grisly work. So there was no further description for the Police to go on. Every policeman who could be spared joined in the hunt, but they had no idea what kind of man they were looking for, beyond the fact that he was 'young-looking' and white, and thought to be fairly presentably-dressed and of medium height. That description could apply to millions of Americans . . .

The area was densely populated. No robberies had been committed at the premises, so this killer would be very difficult to trace. But he must be caught before he killed again, as he most surely would. And did. For this was the type of killer that would not stop at one, or two, or even three. One was never enough . . .

How right the Police were was soon – all too soon – proved. For, within the same month, only fourteen days later and not far away in Santa Barbara, the killer struck again. The victim was a Mrs Anna Russell, aged fifty-eight. A landlady who had offered a room to let. A landlady whose brutalized body, stark naked, had been stuffed under a bed in the very room that the would-be lodger was supposed to be taking.

While the frustrated and impotent Police were fuming with rage at being unable to catch this maniac in their midst, Nelson had moved on, this time to Oakland, where about two months later he raped and strangled Mrs Mary Nesbit, fifty-two, leaving her naked body in the same situation as the last victim – stuffed under the bed in the room he had been shown as available to let.

Like all mass murderers, Nelson killed to a pattern. Rarely do mass murderers use varying methods. The poisoner poisons. The knife-wielder stabs. The strangler strangles – he does not shoot. And Nelson was a strangler. The so-called Dark Strangler who was terrorizing California. Widows and other women of slender resources, who had sought to augment their means by taking lodgers, now started taking down the 'To Let' signs from their windows and getting jobs in factories or as waitresses. Every one of the Dark Strangler's five victims had drawn him to her house by the display of a 'Room For Rent' sign. Yet there were landladies unwilling to allow themselves to be stampeded out of their livelihood. After all, they reasoned, there were still plenty of decent young men – students and so on – who genuinely required lodgings. Or, they argued, since the Dark Strangler was said to be a young man, they would take only older men or women. Two more months passed, and there were no more landlady murders in California. Perhaps they could all breathe more easily now, at least in San Francisco, San José, Santa Barbara and Oakland. But not in Oregon . . .

Portland, Oregon, was to be shocked by three landlady stranglings on consecutive days – 19, 20 and 21 October 1926. A few days after advertising her home for sale, Mrs Beatrice Withers, a thirty-five-year-old divorcee with a son of fifteen, was found, her naked body stuffed into a trunk in the attic. She had been raped and strangled. This time a few articles of jewellery were missing, also a coat and a few dollars in cash. This was the first time that theft had accompanied the killing and this time the victim was about twenty years younger than the other victims. Police, not connecting this death with the series of killings in California, at first thought it to be suicide, until someone tersely pointed out that a suicide would be unlikely to rape and strangle herself and then lock herself inside a trunk and throw away the key.

The next day Mrs Virginia Grant, a fifty-nine-year-old widow, who had advertised her house to let prior to moving, was found dealt with in similar fashion, only on this occasion the body had been hidden behind a boiler. Her house was a stone's throw from the house of the previous victim. Despite obvious homicidal appearances, the Police classified this one as death from natural causes! Again it was pointed out that it was unlikely that a person would take off all her clothes and crawl behind a boiler to die – never mind the rape.

One was beginning to wonder just what kind of men were employed in the Police Department of Portland at this time, when the very next day another victim was found, curiously, and perhaps in the circumstances not inappropriately, named Mrs Mabel Fluke. It took this third discovery to make the Police realize that murder was involved. Mrs Fluke had advertised her house to let. Her body was found in the attic and had been treated with more violence than either of the two previous victims. A scarf was knotted tightly round her neck and her rings had been torn from her fingers. The vicious rape had been accompanied by fist blows to the body. A coat and some items of jewellery were missing.

To quote the *Manitoba Free Press* in Canada: 'Slowly the

Police in Oregon have put two and two together . . . perhaps the Dark Strangler is now at work in Portland.' Each victim had advertised her house for sale or rent. The body of each had been hidden. Each had jewellery or watches and a coat taken. Each death had occurred between 12 noon and 3 p.m. (Local newspapers dubbed the strangler 'the Afternoon Killer'.) Some policemen had the temerity to voice the opinion that the Afternoon Killer might be one and the same as the Dark Strangler of California. So they decided to communicate with the San Francisco Police Department about the Bay City killings, requesting details for comparison with their own three cases. And, in the very midst of this inter-departmental consultation, the San Francisco Police were suddenly brought up short by the discovery, on 18 November 1926, of the body of Mrs Wilhelmina Edmunds, fifty-six, who had been advertising her home for rent. The Dark Strangler had nipped back into their territory once again to laugh at them and their pathetic inability to catch him!

The Dark Strangler, however, did not tarry long in the Bay City but made a beeline for Seattle, where Mrs Florence Monks, a wealthy widow who had decided to put her house up for sale and move to Florida was, on 24 November, found strangled and abused by her estate agent who had called to check with her on some legal points. The front door was ajar and the agent thought that she had left the door open for him. The killer had barely enough time to make his getaway, for the body was not even cold when the agent found it, wedged between a kitchen dresser and the stove, rolled up in a mat with the head and legs protruding from the ends. There had been no sign in the window in this case, and it was thought that the killer had seen an advertisement, giving the name and address, in one of the several newspapers in which Mrs Monks had advertised her home. Later it was found that several thousand dollars' worth of jewellery had disappeared from the house.

Portland detective Archibald Leonard was sent by his chief to Seattle to check with that city's Police Department the facts of Mrs Monks's murder and to compare this with the three Portland murders. It is quite possible that the train which carried the detective from Portland to Seattle passed the one carrying Nelson back to Portland, for with a clear ten killings behind him the Dark Strangler now thought it time to return to taunt the Portland Police with yet another killing. This time he chose as his victim Mrs Blanche Myers, forty-eight, and his *modus operandi* more nearly approximated his earlier ones. The 'Room For Rent' sign was still hanging in the window where they found her, strangled with her own apron-strings, her ravaged body hidden under the bed in the room which she had intended to let to the personable, softly-spoken, twenty-nine-year-old would-be lodger, who looked younger than his years . . .

The Portland Police now pulled out all the stops in a frenzied hunt for the Dark Strangler. Every available detective left the case he was working on to devote his sole energies to tracking down the maniac who was terrorizing the hard-working landladies of the Oregon capital. Even deputy sheriffs of adjoining counties were actively enlisted at the expense of seeing to traffic violations, petty thieves and vandals, drunks and disorderlies. The transient population came in for a very hard time: pedlars, beggars, gipsies, tramps, bums and hoboes of all kinds were turned over by the Police without ceremony. Drifters and street people got short shrift. Loiterers stopped loitering abruptly. Even door-to-door salesmen had doors slammed in their faces by hysterical women. Prospective lodgers fared no better, and unless they were at least fifty, or female, went and looked for digs in adjacent towns, even if they were taking up work in Portland. College students, unable to obtain accommodation locally and unable to afford to commute from outlying towns, left their studies and went home. A man between twenty and forty turning up on a woman's doorstep, if he was not known to her, was the signal for a telephone call to the Police, who were deluged with such calls.

The next move by the Portland Police was to issue

descriptions of jewellery stolen from the victims. The day after the murder of Mrs Monks, a man had taken a room at the house of three elderly ladies, and had offered them several items of jewellery for sale at 'bargain' prices. After they had bought them their new lodger had gone out and never came back. The old ladies saw the notice in the local paper carrying photographs of the stolen items, which included several easily-recognizable pieces among the ones they had purchased. They took them straight to the Police. Three of the items proved to have belonged to Mrs Monks. They had also been the first persons to see the 'lodger' clearly, and were able to give the Police a good description of Earle Nelson. The Police put up a reward of 2,500 dollars for his capture and conviction, and circulated his description throughout the US and Canada.

But the Dark Strangler was not to be deterred. He now resurfaced in Council Bluffs, Iowa, and called at the house of unsuspecting Mrs Elizabeth Beard, aged forty-nine, who had a 'Room To Let' sign in her window. She invited him in, which was her undoing. When her married daughter called in the evening with her baby, she found the front door on the latch. She thought this rather odd, as her mother always kept the door locked. Entering the house, she switched on the light . . . Moments later she rushed screaming from the house to the Police station. A police matron held her baby while the young woman sobbed out the details of her dreadful find in the arms of a policeman.

Nelson now decided to take a trip south to Kansas City, where he killed Mrs Bonnie Pace, who at twenty-three was the youngest of his victims so far. Her husband had suggested that they take a lodger to help ends meet. His feelings, after finding his wife's body, stripped, strangled and violated and bundled up in a rug, are more easily conjectured than described. He did not return from work until 10 p.m., several hours after the murder, which gave Nelson ample time to get clear away.

Only four days after killing Mrs Pace on 23 December, Nelson who had barely managed to stifle his fearful compulsion over the Christmas holidays, killed again. Presumably landladies were too busy with family festivities over Christmas to hang out signs for new lodgers, but on 27 December Mrs Germania Harpin, another young landlady of twenty-eight, met the same fate as her predecessor at the hands of the Dark Strangler. She was found, in the same condition, under the bed in her own bedroom, and her eight-month-old baby was found dead in her cot, strangled with a piece of rag. This was the first time Nelson had killed a child, possibly to avoid the child's screaming drawing attention to his activities. Kansas City, after the first benumbing shock, was in uproar. The newspapers castigated the Police for their 'bumbling inefficiency', and other even less complimentary epithets were hurled at them. In fairness to them, they were doing their best, but it is very difficult even for a good police force to catch a phantom who materializes out of nowhere and then disappears into thin air — which was how it seemed to them.

The New Year of 1927 dawned, by which time Earle Nelson had fifteen murders behind him. Even he must have realized that the sands of time were running out for him, and that Nemesis would catch up with him eventually. But, after lying low for four months, he decided to carry on with his murderous rampage. Or perhaps it was not so much a conscious decision as a dreadful compulsion of his dark, disordered mind.

He commenced his 1927 operations in Philadelphia — the 'City of Brotherly Love' — by murdering Mrs Mary McConnell, sixty, who met her end at his hands on 27 April. Her own grandchildren found her body on returning from school. They had been staying with her while their mother was in hospital having a new baby, and later told police how their grandmother had advertised in the local paper for a 'decent young man or student' to take a room in her house to help pay the bills.

From Philadelphia, Nelson made tracks for Buffalo, where he was to commit the first of four horrific murders in just one week. On 30 May he raped and strangled Mrs

Jenny Randolph, thirty-five, who had hung out a window sign. Two days later he killed Mrs Minnie May, fifty-three, and her friend Mrs Atorthy, who lived at the same address, in Detroit. Mrs May's body, naked, strangled and ravished, was found under her own bed, Mrs Atorthy's body, in similar condition, was found partially hidden in a kitchen alcove. It seemed that the killer had been disturbed at his handiwork since he did not complete the hiding of the body (a feature of his M.O.) and he had, apparently, left in a hurry, as the front door was wide open. This quickly drew attention to the fact that all was not well at the house. Neighbours later confirmed to the Police that the two widows had decided to let a room in order to help pay off the mortgage on their house.

It seemed as if Nelson was systematically trying to reduce the landlady population in all the great cities of America – to quote one Detroit newspaper. But Detroit would be spared any further victims. Nelson was already on his way to Chicago. On 3 June Mrs Mary Sietsema, twenty-seven, acquired the dubious distinction of being Earle Nelson's last victim in the United States. This time her husband had not been very keen on the idea of taking a lodger, and had said so in no uncertain terms, but she had gone ahead anyway.

Nelson now made his great mistake – the fatal slip that has trapped many a murderer before and since. He crossed the U.S. border into Canada, and four or five days later reached Winnipeg. This was his undoing.

On 8 June 1927, at 3 p.m., Mrs Catherine Hill, of 133 Smith Street, Winnipeg, rented him a room which she had advertised. He paid one dollar deposit, promising a further sum when he had received his wages from the builder for whom he stated he was working at St Boniface, across the river from Winnipeg. He wanted a quiet room, he said, for religious study. He was carrying a Bible.

Mrs Hill noticed that her new lodger had very strange eyes. They looked very straight at one, and then immediately turned away to look around the room. After chatting with him for some time, however, she did not form an unfavourable impression of the young man. Strange-looking eyes, after all, do not necessarily point to an evil disposition.

Nelson was wearing a blue coat with some buttons missing, dark trousers with blue stripes, and a dusty pair of boots which, according to Mrs Hill, 'looked as if he had been working with lime'. It transpired that in order to reach Winnipeg Nelson had hitched a lift with a John and Mary Hanna at Emerson, at which time he had been wearing a red sweater, tan shoes and a light-coloured cap — the only details they could remember — but they were not certain of the colour of his trousers, or whether he had been wearing a coat or a jacket. In Winnipeg he had gone to the second-hand clothing shop of one Jacob Gerber at 282 Main Street and sold all his own clothes, purchasing the ones which he now wore at Mrs Hill's establishment. In Gerber's shop he had changed into his new outfit, purchasing the items with the money from the sale of his old one.

On the Wednesday night (8 June) Nelson spent the time quietly in his room and did not go out until early next morning. Mrs Hill presumed that he had gone to his work at St Boniface. Later the same day Lola Cowan, the fourteen-year-old daughter of another of Mrs Hill's tenants in the house, was reported missing. Several people went out looking for her, but no trace could be found, and the Police were informed.

At 6 p.m. the same evening (9 June) one William Paterson, of 100 Riverston Avenue, Winnipeg, returned home from work, expecting to find his supper ready, but his wife was nowhere to be found. He assumed that she must have gone to see her sister, who was an invalid, and stayed to supper, although it was most unusual for her to do anything of this kind without leaving a note for him. Perhaps, however, there might have been some emergency. Paterson cooked supper for himself and his two children, aged five and three, who came in from playing with the two children of his next door neighbour, who looked after them while he was at work and his wife was at her part-time afternoon job. She had said something to him a little earlier about giving up this part-time job and taking a lodger instead, so that she could look after their children herself. Her husband had at first demurred, but then decided to leave it to his wife to make her own mind up. A college student, perhaps, might be OK.

By 10 p.m. William Paterson had become anxious about his wife's non-appearance. It was unlike her to stay out so late. It was too far for him to go to her sister's, but he went to the Police to see whether any accident had been reported, and to the local hospital for the same reason, but with negative result. He breathed a sigh of relief. At least she had not been knocked over by a car or a tram, or even a bicycle, in this city traffic.

The children were safely in bed asleep. Paterson decided to take a look around the house, just in case his wife might have left a note in some inconspicuous place and he had overlooked it. In the bedroom he noticed that his suitcase, which was kept locked, had been moved from its usual place. Very odd, he mused to himself. He decided to examine it more closely, and found that the lock had been forced and that some personal belongings, plus 70 dollars in 10 dollar bills, were missing. A hammer was also inside the case which certainly was not there before – it was kept in the coal-shed. Who on earth . . . ? A burglar, obviously.

Paterson was a religious man and knelt in prayer, asking for guidance what to do, more with regard to his missing wife than about the theft. After all, it would be very difficult to catch the thief after this lapse of time, especially if one had no idea what he looked like.

As Paterson started to rise from his knees, he espied the sleeve of a garment under the bed. This was even more odd, because his wife was a very neat and tidy woman and she would never stow clothes for the laundry under the bed, but would drop them into the laundry-basket. The children could not have put anything there either, as they had been next-door from the time his wife would have left for her job. She usually took them next-door, then came back home to prepare the evening meal, short of actually cooking it, before leaving to catch the tram to work. And from 6 p.m. onwards the children had not been in their parents' bedroom at all.

Paterson knelt again to retrieve the garment from under the bed. It was the sleeve of a woman's blouse, and to his horror it contained a hand and arm, cold with the chill of death. He pushed the bedstead to one side and discovered the body of his wife. She was clothed only in the blouse and a petticoat and brassière, all torn. She had been savagely raped and strangled. Her face, head, elbow and hip had been badly bruised, and her wedding ring had been wrenched from her finger. Beside the body were several bloodstained items of men's clothing, including a shirt, but there were none of his wife's undergarments or skirt. Stockings and shoes were still on the body.

Paterson, almost incoherent with grief and shock, summoned the family doctor, a Dr H.M. Cameron, who lived nearby. At first he had thought Mrs Paterson to have been dead for about two hours, but the subsequent post-mortem made him revise his estimate considerably, as it was proved from the medical evidence that she had been killed not later than 3 p.m., most probably between 2 and 3 p.m. This would have been the time when she was in the house after leaving her children with her neighbour, and before going off to her job.

During his preliminary examination of the body, Dr Cameron asked Paterson for the loan of a pen to write his report. Paterson kept a fountain-pen in the breast pocket of a suit which that morning he had left hanging in the closet. Not only was the pen but the suit itself was missing. A shirt was also missing from a drawer.

So now, the Police would know what clothes the murderer would be wearing. That should make the job easier. But as yet, at this early stage, they did not connect this killing with the American murders.

On the Sunday following the murder of Mrs Paterson (June 12) Lola Cowan's body was found under the bed in an unoccupied room in Mrs Hill's house. The murder and rape of this fourteen-year-old child had been more horrific than any of the others, and many of the details were suppressed by the Police. But one thing was now certain: the Dark Strangler had crossed the border between America and Canada. And what he did not know was that he had also crossed the border between immunity and capture.

There was not a town, a village or a hamlet in the whole of Manitoba that was not on red alert for the Strangler. Winnipeg's Police Force mobilized every available man. They had only one object in view – to catch the Dark Strangler at any cost. All forces joined in – city police, provincial police, RCMP and Canadian Pacific Railway Police. Hundreds of civilian volunteers swelled the ranks. Winnipeg was dragged with a fine tooth comb to trace the origin, occupation and whereabouts of every stranger within her gates. Anyone who had arrived in recent weeks was interrogated. Every hotel-keeper, boarding-house proprietor and lodging-house keeper was closely examined.

One of the most marked characteristics of the mass murderer is his strange immunity, despite plentiful and unmistakable clues. There were the clothes he wore when hitching the lift into Winnipeg, sold to Gerber and recognized by another driver who had given him a lift into Emerson. Then there was Paterson's suit and shirt, the discarded one (bought from Gerber) left by the body.

At 1.30 p.m. on the day of the Paterson murder Sam Waldman, the proprietor of a second-hand clothing shop at 629 Main Street, had a customer who wished to change all his apparel for a complete new outfit selected from stock: an overcoat, two-piece suit, shoes, shirt, belt, tie and underwear. He kept only his socks and trousers. The difference in price was 30 dollars in his favour; the Paterson suit had been a good one. He was paid in ten dollar bills, bundled up the spare pair of trousers in a brown paper parcel, and absent-mindedly left behind in the shop his attaché case containing his Bible, the fountain-pen he had stolen from Paterson and various papers which had been in Paterson's locked box. Waldman also found a cigarette-case in the pocket of the exchanged suit jacket. It bore the initials E.N.

The customer, who was unshaven, said that he did not know the city and asked Waldman to direct him to a barbershop. Waldman took him personally across the road to the Central Barbershop at 612 Main Street. Nick Tabor, the proprietor, shaved Nelson, gave him a face massage and a haircut. He noticed scratches on his scalp, blood matting his hair, as he gave him a shampoo. Asked how he got them, Nelson replied that he had been in a fight in a tavern. Nelson paid the barber with a 10 dollar bill. After visiting the barber Nelson bought a new hat and a cap from Chevrier's, a nearby store, and gave his old cap to an old man named Abraham Hofer on a tram.

From the tram terminus at Headingly, Nelson now got a lift from a man named Hugh Elder who was driving to Portage. Nelson told Elder that his name was Walter Woods. The next day, 11 June, which was a Saturday, he arrived in the town of Regina where, calling himself Harry Harper, he engaged a room with a Mrs Rowe at 1852 Lorne Street. Going into the room to negotiate terms with Mrs Rowe, he was frustrated in his purpose by the presence of another woman there, whose surname was, coincidentally, Nelson. He then accosted a small girl on 12th Avenue the same evening, but a woman passerby came and rescued her.

On the following Monday, 13 June, he changed hats at a store at the corner of Broad Street and 11th Avenue, leaving behind his beige felt hat bearing the name of Chevrier's on the lining. The new hat had a tan-coloured band. He then visited Fred England, a jeweller, to whom he sold Mrs Paterson's wedding ring for three and a half dollars, saying, 'My wife and I have just gotten divorced.'

Nelson did not hang about long enough in Winnipeg to arouse suspicion. By 10 a.m. he was already two miles out of the city having left his old clothes in a cupboard at Mrs Rowe's. He got a lift from a salesman named Davidson as far as the town of Davin, where he managed to effect yet

70

a further change of clothing. This time he went in for blue boiler overalls, a khaki shirt and an old black cloth cap. The shabbier and less conspicuous, and the more workmanlike his outfit, the more likely he would be to be taken for just that – an ordinary workman going about his business.

A mile and a half south of Davin, Nelson got another lift for two miles further along the road to Arcola from a salesman named Wilcox on his way to Vibank. A further lift was not forthcoming until 5 or 6 p.m., when one Isidor Silverman took him the remaining thirty miles to his destination, Arcola. During the journey the two men became on friendly terms, so much so that they stayed at the same hotel in Arcola where Nelson registered as 'Virgil Wilson'. The next morning they set off for Delaraine where again they stayed the night in the same hotel, this time in the same room, probably more for economic reasons than anything. The next day they went on to Boissevain where the unlikely duo separated. Nelson told his companion that he was looking for farm work in the district.

At about 5 p.m. Nelson entered the store and post office at Wakopa kept by one Leslie Morgan. He bought cheese, cigarettes and Coca-Cola. Morgan immediately recognized him from his description and photograph in the Winnipeg newspapers, which said that he was wanted not only for two murders in Canada but twenty in the United States. However, there was some delay before Morgan was able to telephone the Police, because the mail train was due and he had to collect the mail bags for his post office. This done, he called the Police immediately and told them the direction in which the fugitive had gone. The Police caught up with him between Wakopa and Bannerman.

Constable Gray took the Dark Strangler into custody. He was wearing the same clothes except that he had changed his soft hat for a straw one. Nelson told the constable that his name was Virgil Wilson, that he hailed from British Columbia and was working in the district for a rancher named George Harrison. Enquiries proved that there was no such person in the area. He was taken back to Wakopa and put into jail at Killarney. The same night he picked the lock with a nailfile and escaped.

The search which now ensued was unparalleled in Manitoba police history. Killarney and its immediate vicinity were transformed into an armed camp. Women and children took refuge in a barricaded church hall. Men armed with guns, pitchforks, anything they could lay their hands on, joined in the chase. Police were rushed from Winnipeg by special train.

Nelson's first thought was a change of clothing. It seemed that he placed his reliance on this as a change of identity. He broke into the house of William Allen, a quarter of a mile from the jail and stole a green sweater and a pair of boots. This did him little good as in such an open area he could not hope to remain at large for long, especially with so many people determined to capture him at all costs. After some hours in the open, his clothes rumpled and soiled, his boots muddy and his hands and face dirty, a man named Alfred Wood met him as he trudged dispiritedly along the road. Wood, who thought he was a tramp, asked him if he had been out all night. Nelson replied that he had slept in the bush. Wood then gratuitously informed him that a special train was due from Winnipeg with Police and dogs to hunt a murderer who had escaped from jail the previous night. But it was already too late to flee. As Nelson was still walking along chatting with Wood, a police car cruised alongside and four officers grabbed him and bundled him into it, still talking. But it had been a pretty close thing: the place where he was recaptured was but four miles from the U.S. border.

The trial of the Dark Strangler opened on Tuesday 1 November 1927 before Mr Justice Dysart. Crown counsel were Mr R.B. Graham, KC and his junior Mr T.W. Laidlaw. Nelson was defended by Mr J.H. Stitt, with Mr J.R. Young as his junior.

Nelson was accused only of two murders, those of Mrs Paterson and Lola Cowan in Canada. Public interest was roused to a fever-pitch of excitement as milling crowds packed the courtroom and stood shoulder to shoulder in all the corridors, hoping for a glimpse of the man who for sixteen months had kept a whole continent in terror.

The sight of the vast crowd had a sobering effect on Nelson, who trembled perceptibly as he emerged from the jail, evidently apprehensive that the crowd would harm him, and he was greatly relieved when he entered the court building, flanked by several policemen. 'Gee, I'm glad to be inside again,' he told one of his guards. 'That sure was *some* crowd!' He was just as nervous when taken back to his cell, and kept close to the officers escorting him.

In the courtroom, however, Nelson was very calm. He sat quietly with his arms folded, but later he took a more obvious interest in the proceedings, especially when the jury were called into the jury-box. He was dressed in a slate-grey suit, a cream shirt and a polka-dot tie, and a pair of black oxfords which had been highly polished. He chatted freely with Constables Sampson and Outerson, two of the officers who had captured him, and who were also on board the train which had brought him back to Winnipeg, 'I'm glad to see you again, boys,' was his cheery greeting.

The process of jury selection in Canada is much more complicated than in Britain, more approaching the American system. By the end of the first day only four members had been empanelled, but by the following day the full jury had been empanelled and most of the prosecution witnesses had been disposed of. Even the appearance of Mrs Fabian, the aunt who had brought him up, left him quite unmoved. She was to be one of the only two defence witnesses.

The trial lasted five days, during which time Nelson spoke only fourteen words. When, on the Thursday, the proceedings proper began and no fewer than twenty witnesses testified against him, Nelson took even less interest than when the trial had started. He sat all day long with his eyes closed, as though asleep, and appeared palpably bored by the proceedings, betraying no outward sign that he was facing a fight for his very life. The only time his expression changed was when he showed obvious pleasure at being taken back to his cell.

The prosecution confined themselves to plain statements of fact, each one a link which, when connected to another, furnished a chain of evidence so complete that the proof of his guilt was unassailable. The defence, therefore, had a most difficult task. Mr Stitt and his junior, Mr Young, realized early that their one frail hope of saving the life of their client was to plead insanity, but here, as has been the case with many others both before and since, the difficulty lay in the great latitude in the legal interpretation of that term.

Mrs Fabian's evidence was given in a quiet and gentle manner. She said that her nephew appeared to have no sense of moral responsibility at all, citing examples such as when he would tell her that he was going to work, although she knew that he had no job, and that he would come back two hours or so later. 'He was jealous of all my friends,' she continued, 'especially if I were to pass the time of day with a man. He was even jealous of my women friends. Soon I was quite afraid to look at anybody. He was even jealous of tram-conductors to whom I paid fares, and would make a scene.'

Mrs Fabian, however, was also at pains to draw the court's attention to Nelson's good points, such as the occasion when he gave a blood transfusion which saved her life when she had been in St Mary's Hospital in San Francisco. However, his conduct in the hospital during visiting hours left much to be desired, and the hospital staff soon considered him to be very mentally abnormal and eccentric. He used to get very annoyed when his aunt told him that he had to leave because visiting time had ended, and he accused her of wishing to get rid of him so that she could carry on an affair with a doctor. Often he would sit at her bedside and just gaze vacantly into space for long periods without saying a word.

She said that at home he would sit for two or three hours at a time in an apparent daze, not knowing where he was

74

or what he was doing; even his eyes appeared to take on a different colour. He looked, she said, like a person under the influence of drugs, although she had no proof that he was taking any.

One day Nelson told his aunt that he was tired of living in her house, and when asked why, he said that 'everybody there was against him' – a strange statement indeed, since Mrs Fabian went out to work to support him and the only other members of the family were her two children, aged seven and nine. He said that he wished to purchase a house for himself, and went to an estate agent. When the latter asked him what deposit he was prepared to put up for such a purchase, it transpired that all he had in the world was two dollars . . .

When Nelson and his aunt were out together, her evidence continued, he would frequently stop abruptly and walk off without telling her where he was going. He also seemed to suffer from periodic amnesia, and there were occasions when she was afraid of what he might do. On one occasion, saying that he was going to take a bath, he took a glass of water and poured it over his feet. 'He did not even take off his shoes and socks first,' she added. He had bizarre eating habits, even in public. One day he went into a restaurant and ordered a dish of prunes and a glass of water, while on another occasion he ordered a dish of strawberries with a fried egg on top. The record does not say whether the waiter complied. He liked to wear freakish clothing and at one time took to wearing a golf suit, although he never played golf. Once he dressed in white from head to foot; on yet another occasion he posed as a university student and dressed in the garb of an undergraduate.

Mrs Fabian stated that he had several times threatened to commit suicide, saying that the whole world was against him (a typical manifestation of advanced paranoia). Yet, despite all his oddities, she said that he seemed to be very religious-minded and appeared to have a very good knowledge of the Bible, which he could quote at length, citing chapter and verse. She treated him more as a child than as an adult, considering him to be 'a bit mental, but harmless'. She could not believe that he had committed murder.

While the defence admitted that their only possible hope was to try to convince the jury that the murders had been committed during a spell of complete madness, Mr Graham, for the prosecution, had a less hypothetical aspect of the case to put before the jury – one that was much more likely to appeal to the status of the body of men who made up the jurors. Seven were farmers; the others comprised a chauffeur, a mechanic, a warehouseman, a fireman and a steelworker. Such down-to-earth working men were unlikely to know a great deal about psychology or psychiatry, or to have the type of unduly imaginative mind given to flights of fancy. 'It is the part of Crown counsel to put before you, cold-bloodedly, carefully and scrupulously, the evidence before you for and against the accused,' said Mr. Graham. He then went on to give a definition of circumstantial evidence that would be difficult to improve upon: 'My learned friend Mr. Stitt used the words "the chain of circumstantial evidence". Circumstantial evidence, members of the jury, is not a chain – it is a rope, which is not as strong as its weakest strand only, but has the stength of all its strands combined. In the story of this crime, how thoroughly the evidence is borne out and amplified by the details, weaving all together in such a way that every strand has been spun out and bound and twisted with its fellow strands into a cord that is almost perfect!' This simile is as exact for the student as it was unfortunate for the prisoner. It was with this cord, woven from the innumerable strands of circumstantial evidence, that Earl Nelson was hanged.

On the following day the judge delivered his summing-up with an obvious sense of the weight of responsibility with which he was charged. According to the judge, not the accused's guilt but only his sanity could be called into question. To establish a defence on the ground of insanity, he said, it must be actually proved that a man was labouring under a defect of reasoning and that he did not know that he was doing wrong. In coming to a conclusion upon this question of sanity, the judge asked the jury to bear in mind the accused's constant changes of clothes, his changes of name, and his movements . . . 'Read these acts,' the judge said, 'and try to discern from them whether they are the acts of an insane man, irresponsible in the eyes of the law, or the acts of a man who has done some wrong and is trying to escape the consequences.'

The jury found Earle Nelson guilty, and few persons in that packed courtroom thought that they would do otherwise. Asked whether he had anything to say before sentence was passed, he merely stated that he was not guilty of the crimes with which he had been charged. Asked if there were anything further he wished to say, he replied, 'No, not that I know of.'

While sentence was pronounced Nelson stood to attention in soldierly fashion, though when Mr Justice Dysart came to the words 'taken from the place from whence you came' Nelson was seen to swallow nervously, but when the judge said the words 'hanged by the neck until you are dead' the prisoner had recovered all his previous indifference and was apparently unconcerned. His first words on being returned to his cell were to ask for better food.

There is reason to believe that the twenty-two murders enumerated in this account do not necessarily cover the whole story of Nelson's career. Strong circumstantial evidence points to the conclusion that in Newark, New Jersey, in 1926 Nelson was responsible for the triple murder of Mrs Rose Valentine, Mrs Margaret Stanton and Mrs Laura Tidor. All were landladies, all were raped and strangled and two of their bodies were found hidden under their beds. The third was left in a bedroom rolled up in a rug – almost a carbon copy of the Pace and Monks killings.

Nelson never confessed to any of his murders. Interviewed

by a newspaper reporter on the day before his execution, he was asked if he had anything to confess to get off his conscience. 'I have never committed murder,' replied the prisoner. 'Why should I lie? Tomorrow I am going to hang anyway.' He added that he had never been anywhere east of Nevada until he came to Winnipeg, nor had he ever visited most of the cities in which the crimes had been committed. He even repudiated his own handwriting on postcards he had sent to his aunt from Philadelphia at the time of the McConnell killing on 27 April of the previous year, saying that the cards were the work of a forger.

When he was shown a wrist watch that had been stolen from the McConnell house at the time of the murder and sold in New York by a man whom the jeweller positively identified as Nelson from police photographs, he said he had never seen it before.

The husband of Mrs McConnell, and the parents of Lola Cowan were allowed to visit the prisoner in the condemned cell. To all three he protested his innocence. 'I am not guilty,' he said, 'I did not commit these or any other murders. Tomorrow they will hang an innocent man.'

The Dark Strangler was hanged at 7.41 a.m. on 13 January 1928. As two guards led him through the prison yard to the gallows, his iron nerve and studied calm which had characterized his demeanour throughout his trial did not fail him. He walked unassisted up the steps of the scaffold, and although pale he seemed perfectly composed. Half-way up the ladder he seemed to falter, but only for a moment or two. As he stood on the trapdoor, his head thrown back in bold relief against a leaden sky, he made a brief statement denying all guilt of the crimes for which he had been sentenced, 'I declare my innocence before God and man,' he said in a clear, strong voice, 'I forgive those who have injured me, and I ask pardon from those I have injured. May the Lord have mercy on my soul.'

A psychiatrist might perhaps infer that the memory of

his hideous crimes was so disturbing, so painful to the killer that afterwards they became relegated to his subconscious and blotted from his awareness in a kind of retrograde amnesia. Be that as it may, no one thought it just a coincidence that after the Dark Strangler's execution no more landladies were found under the bed.

# CHAPTER SEVEN

## Heads You Lose

School was out, and before going home Jacob Morrow and his friend Jonathan Stern, both fourteen, decided to go and rummage for discarded bottles among the trash on Jackass Hill, a rubbish-dump not far from their school in Cleveland, Ohio. The dump was a weed-choked wasteland, overgrown with bushes and scrub and littered with refuse of every description. Soon both boys had gathered a quantity of soft drink bottles which they could return to local shops for a refund on the deposits, and each boy would have a tidy sum to augment his pocket-money.

'You coming, Jake?' Jonathan called out, 'I'm ready to go home now for my tea.'

'Trust you, always thinking about your stomach!' his friend laughed. 'I'm just going to have another look over here, then I'm ready.' And he scampered over to look among some bushes.

Jonathan had already turned towards the homeward path, when suddenly he heard a shout from Jacob. But it was not the normal shout of a boy calling to his buddy – it was a shout of horror.

'What is it?' Jonathan cried as Jacob rushed towards him in panic, dropping his paper bag and scattering bottles in all directions.

'There's a man's body in the bushes!' Jacob gasped. 'Its head has been cut off!' His breath came in agonized gulps as he strove manfully to conquer the rising tide of nausea that threatened to overcome him.

'We'd better tell someone,' Jonathan said, half wondering at first whether to believe his friend or not, but soon realizing that it must be true, because his pal was making valiant efforts not to be sick. They spotted a man walking his dog and decided to stop him as he was the first person they saw. 'We've found a body in the bushes without a head!' they told him.

At first the man thought they were kidding, but soon he realized that the boys were serious and went with them to check their find. A decapitated, nude male body lay in the bushes, just as they had said. 'We'll go straight to the Police,' the man said. 'You two had better come along too, of course. The Police will want to take statements from you as being the first to find the body.'

Two officers were soon at the scene and they searched the site carefully, in the meantime sending for reinforcements to rope off the area to preserve any evidence. Quite soon, another male body was found, about thirty feet away from the first; this body was also naked, except for a pair of cotton socks. The corpse was similarly decapitated. The Police continued their search of the site and found a shallow grave in the sandy soil. From this they uncovered the head of a middle-aged man, and a little distance away they also unearthed the head of a younger man.

By this time Cleveland Police were diligently combing the entire hillside site. They found half-buried clothing, including underwear, a coat, and a stained white shirt. The label attached to the coat bore the name of a high-class menswear store in Cleveland. The garments were bloody, indicating that the men had been murdered while dressed and their clothing subsequently removed.

The bodies and heads were transported to the city morgue and after a preliminary examination the coroner informed reporters that the older man, around forty-five-years-old and five feet six inches in height, had been dead about a week, and that some kind of chemical had been poured over the body, staining it a deep brown. The younger man, he said, was in his early thirties, and had been dead not more than two or three days at most. The condition of both bodies established that they had been decapitated while still alive, and that this decapitation had been a thorough job by someone with anatomical knowledge. The victims' limbs had also been tied.

The murders created a wave of horror throughout Cleveland and the entire state of Ohio. Newspapers were quick to report the usual 'monster at large' stories. The younger victim was identified first. He was Edward Andressy, an orderly at the City Hospital, who lived with his parents on Cleveland's West Side. Police records showed that he had one conviction for carrying a concealed weapon in a public place. He had a scar on his forehead and an appendix operation scar on his abdomen. His dental record was also found and this clinched the identification.

Relatives of the dead man informed Detective Inspector C.W. Cody that he had been missing for ten days or so. One witness said, 'Ed had been afraid to go out for several days', but no explanation as to why was forthcoming. He was also known to have been warned by an angry husband to 'keep away from his wife, or else', but no one knew the woman's identity. These threats were followed up by the Police. Assistant Chief Inspector Emmet J. Potts sent them to the Kingsbury District Police Precinct where the woman was thought to reside, but they failed to discover either the woman's identity or that of her husband. And, while these inquiries were going on, there was still no clue as to the identity of the older victim.

Four months passed, and the city of Cleveland slowly recovered from the horror of the murders. Then, at the end of January 1936, a security guard on duty in the grounds of a factory heard a dog barking excitedly near a recess in the factory building and went to investigate. He found two canvas bags and a basket hidden in the recess. Curious as to their contents, he pushed aside the barking dog and looked inside. To his horror, he found parts of a dismembered body. The bags contained a right hand and a right arm and the basket contained a woman's thighs.

The district in which the security guard made his gruesome discovery was situated just on the border of the Kingsbury district. The news media revived the notion of a ghoul at work in Cleveland, but despite the most intense police activity not a single clue was found. Two weeks later, a lorry driver looking into some rubbish behind a derelict building in Orange Avenue uncovered the left arm and lower legs of a female. The lorry driver was less self-controlled than Jacob Morrow – he was violently sick. Then he called the Police.

After his preliminary examination, the coroner announced that both these finds were connected. He told a shocked gathering of news reporters that the body had been dismembered only two or three days previously. However, identification was soon to follow. A clear thumbprint was obtained from the severed right hand, and George J. Koestler, Chief of the Police Bureau of Criminal Investigation, who had 12,000 thumbprints on record, checked them and found the one he was looking for about three-quarters of the way through them. It belonged to Mrs Florence Sawdey Polillo. Her husband was traced to Buffalo, and was eliminated from the inquiry. Her head was never found.

In June of the same year, two boys were playing football on some waste ground in Kingsbury when they found a bundle consisting of a rolled-up pair of men's trousers tied round with string. Being inquisitive like all young boys, they untied the string and opened the bundle – and a man's head rolled out. Shrieking, they ran for a policeman.

A search was instituted over the entire area within a half-mile radius of the place where the boys had found the head. The next day the body belonging to the head was found, 200 yards from where the boys had played. The body was covered with tattoos, including the names Helen and Paul, a dove, a cupid and an anchor. Was he a sailor? He was aged about twenty-five, and had been decapitated while alive not more than three days previously. He could have been a seaman working steamers plying the Great Lakes.

A death mask was made from the face and a photograph published in an effort to ascertain his identity, but this drew a complete blank. Surely someone must know this young man? It seemed not – he was probably a transient from out of state.

Less than a month later a nude male body, *sans* head, was found floating in a West Side creek, some distance from the by now notorious Kingsbury district. Horror was now mounting in Cleveland. The newsmen were right – a monster was truly at large in their midst.

Then, in mid-September – almost a year after the finding of the first two victims by Jacob Morrow and Jonathan Stern on Jackass Hill – the Kingsbury district surrendered another partial male body which was found under a weed-choked bridge by a woman exercising her two dogs. This victim too, remained unidentified.

Some months later a mutilated torso was found in the icy waters of Lake Erie. Medical experts could say only that it was the torso of a young woman and that she had been pregnant, but this victim also proved impossible to identify.

In mid-June 1937 a young boy idly throwing stones into the Cuyahoga River had the shock of his life. Ripples bounced an object against a bridge a few feet away. As the water ceased swirling, the boy could see the top of a human skull. Investigating further, he found a skeleton enclosed in a sack. Police called to the scene found pieces of a soiled and stained newspaper which, when cleansed and flattened in the forensic laboratory, proved to be part of the Cleveland *Plain Dealer*, a popular Midwest paper. What was of particular interest, however, was the fact that this contained a review of a movie. One of the detectives on the case, Peter Merylo, thought that this review might provide a clue. It did. He checked with all first-run movie houses in the area, since only the first showing of a film gets into the reviews in the *Plain Dealer*. At the Palace Theatre, the film described had been showing from 5 to 11 June 1936, and the elusive 'Headhunter' (as the Press described him) was thought to have been active in the days following early

June 1936. The newspaper had been soaking in the sack for almost a year, until it was found. Three gold teeth were also found in the lower left jaw, and Police were still trying to trace their owner through dental records when further grisly relics surfaced in the Cuyahoga River. These were the dismembered parts of a male body, about thirty-five years of age, but they, too, proved impossible to identify.

The Police were stymied. They were beside themselves with frustration. The citizenry of Cleveland was outraged. Neighbour was suspicious of neighbour. The Press had a field-day with their descriptions of the unknown murderer: monster, cannibal, ghoul, vampire, and so on. The grim saga had gone on like a macabre serial story for over a year. And it had not ended.

On a beautiful spring day in 1938, just as Cleveland was beginning to resume a more normal life and hope that the nightmare was behind them, the sluggish waters of the Cuyahoga gave up another sack containing the torso and left foot of a woman and also an unwrapped lower leg. In the morgue, forensic examination soon proved these to be parts of the same body. The woman was a mature blonde and her headless condition proved to be once more the grisly hallmark of the mysterious executioner who now had Cleveland in a grip of terror.

The coroner recorded a significant oddity. The severed leg had been cleanly dissected at knee and ankle joints, while the remainder found in the sack seemed to have been dismembered with greater haste, as though carried out immediately after death and with less deliberation, though still with the customary familiarity with the knife and skill in handling it. Had the murderer been disturbed at his grisly handiwork? If so, had anyone seen or heard anything unusual in the vicinity?

The numbers of victims had now reached double figures. A Press conference was convened, at which Police Chief George J. Matowicz described how his men had interviewed no fewer than 1,500 persons. Many criminals had been rounded up in the district – he had 'dry-cleaned the underworld', as Chief Matowicz put it. Forty-seven mentally-disturbed persons had been taken into custody; some were known to be capable of violence or could be potential killers judging from their past histories. Unregistered aliens, as well as known sex perverts, were also rounded up. But despite this massive operation, no useful leads turned up. There was just no indication that the killer had been caught in the dragnet of the law. Glumly, Chief Matowicz was unable to offer the Press any hope, or promise that any arrest would be made in the foreseeable future.

Detective Merylo, still checking dental records, learned of a woman who had been missing since June 1936, although there had been no mention of her case at headquarters. A further check of the skeleton found in the Cuyahoga River proved to be that of the missing woman, Mrs Rose Wallace, aged forty, a widow, of Scotville Avenue. The reason Merylo had had no luck checking Cleveland dentists was because Mrs Wallace had attended a dentist in Cincinnati.

In mid-August a young man was walking along Lake Shore Drive when his attention was caught by something unusual. Upon checking he found lying among some rocks a partially unwrapped brown paper parcel; it was this paper, flapping in the breeze, which had caught his eye. Looking into the parcel, he vomited at the sight of a dismembered and decapitated female body; again it was nude. The severed head was lying beside the body. When he had regained his equilibrium, he went to the Police to report his grisly find.

The woman, a blonde, was about thirty-five years of age, five feet five inches tall and 125 pounds. In the parcel with the body was a popular weekly magazine dated 5 March 1938. Police searched the Lake Shore Drive area thoroughly and this search produced the body of the twelfth and last known victim of the elusive Headhunter. Almost disintegrated, it had been in its shallow grave for several months, possibly longer. The skull, with hair attached, was present, together with about forty bones from various parts of the body. Careful reconstruction in the forensic laboratory estimated that it was the body of a male, aged between forty-five and fifty. The body had been wrapped in an old quilt, which was photographed by the Police so that a picture could be published in the local newspapers. Someone, somewhere, might have seen such a quilt, or even owned it, and could prove a vital witness.

Chief Matowicz received a call from a Cleveland barber who told him that he had come to identify the quilt, which looked like one he had sold to a totter some time previously. Hours later, a very surprised totter was stopped on his round by the Police and asked some pointed questions. Yes, he had bought a tattered old quilt like the one in the police photograph from the barber, and had sold it in his turn to a waste rag processing firm. The firm, when seen by the Police, could not help: the quilt had been stolen from their yard several weeks previously. Matowicz was disappointed that this promising new lead had petered out, but he was not unduly discouraged. Sooner or later he felt sure another clue would surface and lead him to the killer.

A private investigator friend of Sheriff O'Donnell, of Cuyahoga County, voiced the opinion that the Police should consider three points in looking for the killer's place of operations, for it was inconceivable that he could have butchered the bodies at the places where they were found. First of all, the investigator said, the scene of operations would have to be soundproof; secondly, it would have to be furnished with refrigeration for the storage of dismembered body parts; and thirdly, the place would have to be capable of being kept generally clean and tidy so as to avoid arousing the suspicions of neighbours or other persons. Up to now, there had been absolutely no reports whatever of anyone hearing screams or shouts, or seeing blood or anything else suspicious – the ogre left no traces of his activities.

The point about refrigeration in particular aroused Sheriff O'Donnell's interest. After consultations with his deputies, a team visited ice-cream warehouses, meat-packing factories, breweries and cold-storage plants. The visits were attended by a singular lack of success. Unlike Matowicz, O'Donnell was discouraged. This idea had not worked out, so instead he decided to concentrate on people rather than places. He put some men undercover to visit saloons and bars in the Kingsbury district in order to locate anyone who had known those victims whose identities were confirmed. O'Donnell's private investigator friend joined the undercover team.

The indefatigable private investigator managed to find a bar where two of the Headhunter's known victims, Edward Andressy and Rose Wallace, had both been regular patrons. No one in the bar itself seemed to know much about them or their backgrounds, so O'Donnell instituted house-to-house inquiries in the immediate vicinity of the bar. At one house a man who worked as an itinerant fruitseller mentioned a man named Frank who was inordinately interested in knives, and possessed some unusually large ones: 'You know, like butchers' knives. Real biggies. But he's a bricklayer. What would a brickie want with big knives? That was all he ever talked about.'

Discreet inquiries were made about 'Frank', who was indeed a bricklayer by trade, but he had been in and out of twelve different jobs in the past year for no reason that even the Police could satisfactorily discover. The inquiries into 'Frank's' background narrowed to a city block in the 1900 region of Central Avenue – a convenient walking distance from the bar frequented by the first and eighth victims, Edward Andressy and Rose Wallace. It was also not far from the areas where some of the gruesome relics of other victims had been found.

The man the police were seeking was named as Frank Dolezal, but he had moved from the address. Some intensive questioning of neighbours ferreted out his new address, a four-roomed apartment not far away. The apartment was empty when the Police visited it, and they decided to search it thoroughly. No clues were found until they reached the bathroom. On examining this they found long-dried traces of blood that had filled cracks in the floorboards and other uneven surfaces (the building was an old one).

The blood proved to be human. O'Donnell then organized a further search even more thorough than the first. This proved more successful. Hidden in a 'safe' place, behind some wall-boarding, the officers found four large butchers' knives. Two had minute traces of dried human blood at the joint between haft and blade. With this evidence the Police could now move in to arrest the man who had held Cleveland in the grip of fear for more than two years.

Dolezal, now fifty-two, had emigrated to the USA at the age of sixteen. He was stocky, physically strong, with pale blue eyes which were well spaced, giving him an alert look. He had been a sailor and bore a number of tattoos. At one time he had worked in a slaughter-house, but had latterly gone back to brick-laying, his usual trade. The Police decided to stake out the apartment and arrest him on his return from work. He submitted without a struggle.

The shock announcement was delayed until late at night when Dolezal was safely in custody and it made coast-to-coast news. Taken to Cuyahoga County Jail, he asked to take a lie detector test, but was refused. He denied all guilt and professed no knowledge of the killings apart from what he had read in the newspapers. He admitted only to having assaulted a woman while he was drunk and because she had tried to take 10 dollars from his pocket. Large crowds demonstrated outside the jail and his fellow prisoners made their point with noisy bangings and shoutings and yells of 'Cannibal!'

At a preliminary hearing, the coroner pointed out the pattern running through all the twelve known killings. All victims had been left naked; all had been beheaded; all the bodies had been left in rags or paper. Dismemberment was always cleanly through the joints; no bones had been sawn or broken. Dr Strauss, the forensic pathologist, and Dr O'Malley, the police surgeon, agreed that Dolezal was a butcher rather than a surgeon, and that his having formerly worked in an abattoir was significant, as it had provided him with a good knowledge of anatomy and of how and where to sever limbs in the easiest and cleanest way.

Rags were used by Dolezal in the disposal of his victims, and rags played a part in his own death. He never came to trial, for one day guards found him hanged in his cell. He had fashioned a rope from rags.

# CHAPTER EIGHT

## Born to Raise Hell

Chicago has had perhaps more than its fair share of crime, but the mass-murder of eight young nurses in one night, in 1966, rivals even the St Valentine's Day massacre in 1929, when seven gangsters were lined up in a garage on Clark Street and shot to death by four rival gangsters. But that can scarcely be compared to this, the bloodiest mass-murder in Chicago's history. The one was a cold-blooded execution carried out in the interests of power and profit; the other was the senseless savagery of a bloodlust-crazed psychotic.

Richard Franklin Speck was born on 6 December 1941, the son of Benjamin Speck, a potter, and his wife Mary Margaret. He was one of eight children. From Kirkwood, Illinois, the family moved to Monmouth, in the same state, where they lived until 1947 and then moved to Dallas, Texas, where Richard graduated at the J.L. Long Junior High School in the eighth grade, but did not continue his education beyond this point. In 1951 he married Shirley Malone, who was only fifteen at the time. A daughter was born to them, but the marriage did not last.

Speck was six feet one inch tall, blond-haired and blue-eyed, slender in build and thin-faced, but his most distinctive feature was a tattoo 'Born to Raise Hell' on his left forearm. He used several aliases at various times: Richard Benjamin Speck, Richard Franklin Lindbergh, B. Bryan, among others – but that tattoo would always identify him, whatever name he used. When he worked, he was usually a garbageman, or, on occasions, a crew member aboard freighters plying the Great Lakes; but he worked only when he felt like it – and when he was not locked up by the Police.

His record shows that he was arrested ten times in Dallas, while still under twenty years of age, on charges of trespass, disorderly conduct and burglary. Before coming to Chicago in 1966 he had had a total of thirty-seven arrests and was still wanted for burglary in Dallas. By the time he had drifted back to Illinois from Texas he was well versed in violent crime and by the spring of 1966 he was a chronic drunk and a 'speed freak' (amphetamine addict). Later he was to attribute his violent nature and criminal conduct to several blows on the head which he had sustained during fights in taverns, throwing in alcoholism, drug addiction and a deprived childhood in a poor home for good measure. When sober, which was not very often, he used to spend most of his time looking at comics and cartoon strip magazines, since he could not read. Almost totally illiterate, he could barely sign his name – or one of his aliases.

Early in 1966 Speck was working as a seaman aboard an ore boat on Lake Superior. He had an attack of appendicitis which saw him hospitalized in Hancock, Michigan, and while recovering there he spent a good deal of his time with twenty-eight-year-old Judy Laakaniemi, a nurse of Finnish origin, who was later to describe him as 'a gentle and quiet boy' to a friend. Little did she know at that time that only a few months later, in Chicago, he would spend six hours with nine nurses, leaving eight of them dead . . .

At the end of June 1966 Speck was fired from the cargo vessel *Randall* owned by the Inland Steel Company, after fighting with a ship's officer. Unemployed and in need of money, he sought help from one of his married sisters, Mrs Martha Thornton, the wife of a railway worker. She and her husband gave him money and drove him to the National Maritime Union Hiring Hall on 10 July 1966. He expressed a desire to go to New Orleans and attempted to find work aboard a ship destined for that port but there were no available berths. Speck hung around, patronizing several bars used by merchant seamen and drinking very heavily. On 13 July, an acquaintance was later to testify, Speck was 'stinking drunk' and had 'gone on the greatgrandaddy of all benders'. He was also known to have injected himself that night with some kind of drug, although apparently which kind was not known – he used a number of different kinds of drugs.

Eleven p.m. on the night of 13 July saw him lurching unsteadily along East 100th Street, on Chicago's South Side, until he came to a two-storey house, No. 2319, which was one of three houses rented by the South Chicago Community Hospital as a nurses' home. Stopping, he knocked at the front door, at the same time slipping his hands into the pockets of his black jacket and withdrawing a knife and .22 revolver. The door was opened by a pretty twenty-three-year-old Filipino student nurse, Corazon Amurao, who was on a nurses' exchange scheme between the US and the Philippines. Two of her room-mates also accompanied her to the door, wondering who the caller could possibly be at such a late hour. In the statement she made later to the Police she said: 'I opened the door, and a man was standing there. The first thing I noticed about him was that he was reeking of alcohol. Then I saw a gun and a knife in his hands . . .'

'I'm not going to hurt you,' Speck said, 'I'm only going to tie you up. I need your money to go to New Orleans.' He waved the gun about, brandishing the knife and ordered the girls to go upstairs into a rear bedroom where he found three more student nurses. He ordered the six young women to lie down on the floor; seeing the gun and the knife, they had no choice but to obey. Speck tore a sheet from one of the beds into strips and bound each girl hand and foot and stuffed a gag into her mouth. At the same time he kept assuring them that he would not hurt them and that his only intent was to rob.

At 11.30 p.m. Gloria Davy, another nurse, returned from a date. Speck met her at the door and ushered her up the stairs at gunpoint. He did the same when two more nurses,

Suzanne Farris and her friend Mary Ann Jordan, arrived at midnight. All three were bound and gagged. Mary Ann, unlike the other eight girls, did not live at the nurses' home; she had planned to spend the night with her friend, who was soon to become her sister-in-law. Mary Ann's brother was the man Suzanne Farris was going to marry.

Next, Speck asked each girl where she kept her money and they had no choice but to tell him. He systematically took all their available cash and then stood watching his captives for a little time as they stared at him, wide-eyed, from the floor where they lay trussed like chickens. Gloria Davy was considered to be the most beautiful of all the nine girls; Speck looked at her for longer than the others. She was the twenty-two-year-old daughter of a steel company foreman in Dyer, Indiana, one of six children. She had worked as a nurses' aide at the Hospital of Our Lady of Mercy in Dyer and was also president of the Illinois Student Nurses' Association. She had planned to join the Peace Corps after her training programme was completed. It was she who asked Speck, while he was tying her feet, 'Why are you doing this? We are student nurses.' Speck replied, smiling, 'Oh, you are a student nurse? Don't be afraid, I'm not going to kill you.'

When all nine nurses were securely trussed up, Speck got down on the floor and played with the gun and the knife in his hands, talking to the girls all the while. 'Do you know karate?' he asked one of them. He then rose from the floor and kept going to look out of the window. According to the later testimony of Corazon Amurao, he was 'very tense and nervous' at that particular time. He then untied Pamela Wilkening, the twenty-four-year-old daughter of a railway engineer from Lansing, Illinois. A nursing career had always been her life's ambition. Speck led Pamela from the room and a little while afterwards Corazon Amurao heard a deep sigh followed by silence. It transpired that Speck had taken Pamela into another adjoining bedroom and there stabbed her in the left breast. He then twisted a strip of sheet about her neck and strangled her to death, all without speaking a word. From later forensic findings, this murder apparently caused Speck to be sexually stimulated. Although the victim had not been raped or otherwise sexually assaulted, semen was found on the body and on the floor beside it.

But, as with so many psychotics, one killing was not enough . . . Moments later, still brandishing his gun, Speck returned to the rear bedroom and took Mary Ann Jordan and Suzanne Farris to another bedroom. Mary Ann, twenty, was one of the six children of a civil engineer working for the Chicago City Council. Speck lunged viciously at her, stabbing her in the neck, breast and eye, thereby killing her. He then turned his attention to Suzanne Farris, twenty-one and also from Chicago, the daughter of a transit authority worker, one of three children. Suzanne resisted the attack, which infuriated Speck so much that he plunged his knife into her again and again, eighteen times in all, in the back, neck and chin. When she fell upon her back, Speck leapt upon her and strangled her to death, then he tore off her underclothes and ripped them into pieces. After this attack he rose and walked to the bathroom to wash the blood from his hands. Next he went back to the bedroom where the captive girls lay and chose his next victim, Nina Schmale, twenty-four, a tall brunette from Wheaton, Illinois. A former beauty queen, she was the daughter of a cement mason. Before entering the nurses' training course at South Chicago Community Hospital, she had taught Sunday school for four years and also worked as a volunteer nurses' aide in the Du Page Convalescent Home. Her ambition was to pursue a career in psychiatric nursing . . .

Speck ordered Nina to lie down on the bed in yet another of the several adjoining bedrooms. He then stabbed her in the neck and strangled her. He spent from twenty to twenty-five minutes with each victim, carrying out his diabolical acts at a leisurely pace.

The girls remaining still alive in the rear bedroom desperately tried to roll under beds to hide, but none succeeded except Corazon Amurao, who managed to squirm so far beneath one of the beds against the wall that Speck did not spot her. She was the smallest and slenderest of the nine girls. Terrified, she stayed there all night without moving or making a sound; this undoubtedly saved her life.

The next victims were two Filipino girls named Valentina Pasion and Merlita Gargullo. Valentina was twenty-three and came from Jones City in the Philippines; the other girl was twenty-two, the daughter of a doctor from Santa Cruz, in the same country. Both were exchange scheme nurses, like Corazon Amurao. Both had come to the U.S. for the first time one month before the killings. Speck took the two young women into a front-facing bedroom and immediately stabbed Valentina Pasion in the neck, thus killing her. He then stabbed Merlita Gargullo, who fell across the body of her compatriot. Speck then knelt over Merlita's body and strangled her.

Corazon Amurao, from her hiding-place under the bed, heard both girls gasp loudly as they were struck; she also heard Merlita call out a word in her native language, signifying that she was in great pain – equivalent to 'It hurts a lot' – before she died. Speck then again visited the bathroom before returning to the rear bedroom and bringing out Patricia Matusek, twenty, of Czech origin, the daughter of a tavern owner. She was a champion swimmer. Once her training had been completed she intended working in the Chicago Children's Memorial Hospital. She was still bound hand and foot when Speck carried her into the bathroom. Her last words, heard by Corazon Amurao, were, 'Please will you untie my ankles first.' Speck kicked her in the stomach and strangled her to death, leaving her body lying on the floor.

Speck was still not through with his orgy of bloodletting. He returned to the south-facing bedroom; there on the bed lay Gloria Davy. Apparently Speck must have lost count of the original number of girls in the building, his drink-and drug-befuddled brain never missing the petrified Corazon Amurao, who could follow his every move from her place of concealment. The lone survivor later described in court what happened next, 'He stood up, and I could see that he was removing Miss Davy's jeans . . . then I heard his pants being unzipped . . . then when I looked at them I could see that he was already on top of Miss Davy . . .' At this point the witness wept bitterly. 'Then,' she continued, 'I heard the bed springs moving . . . After a few minutes, he asked her, "Will you please put your legs around my back" . . . I heard the movement of the springs for about twenty-five minutes . . . About five minutes after the bed springs stopped moving, I . . . saw that Miss Davy and Speck were not there any more . . .'

Speck had led Gloria Davy naked down the stairs to a front room and ordered her to lie face down on a divan, where he assaulted her again. According to the official forensic report, Miss Davy's rectum had been mutilated, possibly with some kind of sharp-pointed implement. Speck then strangled her with a strip of sheet. Gloria was Speck's last victim, the one he had spent the most time with, and the only one of the eight victims who had been raped.

Yet Corazon Amurao, too, was a victim. Petrified with fear, lying for hours bound, gagged and immobile, stiff from staying in one position and sore from her bonds, she would never forget the horror of that night. She waited until she could hear no more sounds in the house, then she waited some more, to be on the safe side. At 5 a.m. an alarm clock went off in another bedroom, and kept buzzing: it was the usual time for the nurses to rise and get ready for the hospital where they had to report for duty at 6 a.m. Corazon thought that Speck might still be in the building – in a druken stupor, perhaps – so she waited another hour. Then she eased herself gingerly from under the bed and rolled to where she could see to untie her bonds; those on her wrists were not tight enough to stop her from working them loose, whereupon she quickly untied her ankles and the knot of the gag at the back of her head. She then crept quietly along the landing to her own bedroom at the front of the house. As she made her way along she had to step over the bodies of her friends, but she tried to avoid looking at the bloody carnage which surrounded her. Once in the front bedroom, Corazon broke through a screen and crawled out on to a two-foot wide ledge ten feet above the street and began screaming, 'Help me! help me! Everyone is dead! I am the only one alive!'

A neighbour, Mrs Betty Windmüller, and Robert Hall, who was walking his dog, rushed to the front of the building where they saw Corazon cowering on the ledge and screaming hysterically, 'My friends are all dead! All dead! All dead! I am the only one alive! Oh, God! The only one! My friends are all dead!'

Police arrived in minutes and Corazon was rushed to hospital and put under heavy sedation. The first detective to arrive on the scene, Daniel R. Kelly, together with others who joined him soon afterwards, found over thirty fingerprints in the house belonging to the intruder. They also found a man's T-shirt wrapped inside Gloria Davy's white panties. The bedrooms were in wild disarray, with clothing and personal belongings strewn all over the floor and drawers pulled out of chests and upended – obviously in the crazed killer's search for money. None of the girls' handbags or wallets contained any cash. How much had been taken *in toto* could not be determined, but Corazon Amurao told detectives that her own purse had contained thirty-one dollars, which was now missing.

When Corazon was sufficiently recovered to be able to speak coherently she described the mass murderer in detail. A police artist, Otis Rathel, put together a sketch, rather like the British Police Identikit but made up differently, which bore a remarkable likeness to Richard Franklin Speck. This appeared in the next edition of every Chicago newspaper, all of which carried the grisly story of the mass slaying.

Meanwhile the killer had walked to the heart of skid row on Madison Street, where he hit a number of bars. In one of them he heard two men talking about the killings. He turned to them and said, 'I hope they catch the sonofabitch.' Later, Speck claimed that he was not even aware that the Police were looking for him, and that he could not remember anything about the murders.

He spent the next few days drinking incessantly and shooting pool. He also spent some time with a prostitute, to whom he paid three dollars. On 16 July he ended up in the 90-cents-a-night Starr Hotel, a bug-ridden flophouse on West Madison Street, registering under the alias of B. Bryan. Into cubicle number 584 he carried a newspaper folded to reveal a banner headline which read 'Police say nurse survivor can identify killer of 8 nurses.'

Meanwhile, police activity was stepped up throughout the entire city. This man must be caught, and quickly. Forensic findings had shown that Patricia Matusek had been strangled; Pamela Wilkening had been stabbed in the heart and strangled; Nina Schmale had been slashed in the neck and strangled; Valentina Pasion had been stabbed four times and strangled; Mary Ann Jordan had been stabbed three times; Suzanne Farris had been stabbed eighteen times and strangled; Merlita Gargullo had been stabbed and strangled; and finally, Gloria Davy had been raped and sodomized as well as strangled. From this it emerged that all the girls except one had been strangled, and that all except two had been stabbed. It was unusual, to say the least, that the killer should have both stabbed *and* strangled the majority of his victims; most psychotic killers stick to one method of killing.

Corazon Amurao had been able to give the Police a very accurate description of the mass-murderer; she had also spotted his most distinguishing mark, the tattoo 'Born to Raise Hell'. There were also other clues. The hands of the girls had all been tied with the backs of their wrists together and palms facing outwards, the same way a policeman handcuffs prisoners, which suggested an ex-con. The square knots were the kind tied by seamen – the man had spoken of going to New Orleans to find a ship.

This pointed to a distinct line of inquiry. Half a block away from the nurses' home, at 2335 East 100th Street, was the Hiring Hall of the Seamen's Union. Police quickly learned from William O'Neill, the hiring agent, that a pockmarked man with a tattoo had been inquiring about a ship to New Orleans two days earlier and had returned on Wednesday, the day of the murders, to fill in an application form. He had filled in the name of Richard F. Speck, his real name, and had given his married sister as his next of kin, with her address and including also her telephone number. Police also heard that the nurses frequently sunbathed in the rear garden of the nurses' home and that Speck had been seen wandering around in the park behind it hoping for a glimpse of bikini-clad beauties.

The Police rang the number of Speck's sister. Their ploy was to tell her that a job on a ship at the hiring agency was now available. The detective who made the call posed as a clerk from that agency. The next time her brother called her, he said, she was to tell him to call at the hiring agency without delay. Meanwhile the hiring agency and Mrs Thornton's residence were staked out. Speck called his sister and was given the message and promised to be at the agency within an hour, but he failed to turn up. The Police knew that Speck was unquestionably their man, since Corazon Amurao had given them a positive identification of Speck's passport photograph clipped to the application form he had filled in. A copy of this photograph was now in the hands of every team combing Chicago for him.

A seaman who knew Richard Speck also remembered having seen him walking along Crandon Avenue and into Luella Park, where he sat on a bench, ostensibly idly watching children at play on the swings. An alert policeman, having been shown the location of the bench, determined that Speck from this vantage point would have had a clear and unobstructed view of the rear of 2319 East 100th Street, which housed the eight nurses . . .

Detectives began combing the type of lodging-house that sailors frequented. They found a cheap hotel, the Shipyard Inn, on N. Dearborn Street, with Speck's name in the register, but he had checked out half an hour previously.

The following day the officer in charge of the case,

Sergeant of Detectives John Murtaugh, announced on television that the man they wanted to interview was Richard Speck and the suspect's photograph was shown. Speck had now registered in a small room at the Starr Hotel, at 617 W. Madison Street, under the name of B. Bryan. He had spent all the money he had taken from his victims. The rooms were little more than cubicles, eight feet by six feet, with a wire mesh ceiling to keep out petty pilferers. They were furnished with just a cot, a wooden stool and a tin locker. The floor was of concrete, without benefit of mats or rugs. He had paid his last dollar for the night's lodging and received just ten cents in change. Not only money but time too was running out for Chicago's most horrific mass murderer . . .

Speck wanted money for liquor. He annoyed his neighbour in the next cubicle, a man named George Gregorich, by begging him for a few dollars, offering to share the bottle of liquor with him. Speck got short shrift and was forcefully told to leave him alone. At midnight Speck again knocked on the door of Gregorich's room, and Gregorich, by now exasperated by the drunk who was disturbing his sleep, got out of bed and opened the door. As he did so, Speck fell across the theshold into his room, bleeding copiously from slashed wrists. Gregorich ran down the five flights of stairs in his pyjamas to tell the night clerk, William Vaughan, who called an ambulance. The two ambulancemen who responded to the call, Eugene Kraus and Michael Burns, logged the call at 12.45 a.m. and sped to the Starr Hotel. Told that the bleeding man was in Room 584 on the fifth floor, they rushed up the stairs and found Richard Speck lying on the cot, his arms dangling over the sides, spilling blood which ran across the floor. Quickly they tourniqueted his arms and twenty minutes later Speck was in the Cook County Hospital. Dr Leroy Smith, the resident surgeon, found that 'B. Bryan' had severed a vein in his left arm, but that the cut on the right arm was of a more superficial nature. Then, as he was stitching the left arm, he noticed the tattoo, 'Born to Raise Hell'. He had seen the news item about this in his evening paper. As soon as the arm was stitched and bandaged he called a nurse to the casualty room. 'Call the Police,' he said as he started to swab and bandage the injured man's right arm. Speck raised his head and looked at Leroy Smith. 'Do you collect the 10,000 dollars, Doc?' he whispered. Then he relapsed into unconsciousness.

Police quickly posted an armed guard outside the ward cubicle where Speck lay recovering from his self-inflicted wounds. It was just sixty-seven hours since Corazon Amurao had struggled screaming on to the ledge in East 100th Street, after she had climbed over the corpses of eight of her friends . . .

Asked what had happened at the Starr Hotel, George Gregorich told detectives, 'At about midnight this guy came in and fell up against my door, bustin' right through it. I had been tryin' to read earlier and the guy kept annoyin' me all evenin'. Then when I tried to sleep, he started again. I was ready to belt the bum. Then I looked an' I saw the guy was bleedin' like a stuck pig. I lifted him and took him back to his own room and laid him on the bed. Then I ran to get help.' Later, detectives found a bloody broken beer bottle in the men's lavatory adjoining, with a trail of blood leading to Room 584.

Murtaugh was later to recall, 'It had been a quiet night – unusually quiet, and very warm. Ordinarily we would have been jumping, but there was not that much activity that night in the whole area. We got a call. The policeman on the scene said there were five bodies. Later he called back and said six. Still later, eight . . . I then assumed full charge of the scene.' Murtaugh then set in motion what would prove to be the biggest manhunt in Chicago history. He arrived in an unmarked car, accompanied by two detectives, Byron Carlisle and John Wallenda. Their commander, Francis Flanagan, also arrived separately. Murtaugh recalled what followed:

'How bad is it?' Flanagan asked.

'Very bad,' Kelly (the officer first on the scene) replied,

as he led the commander into the ground floor lounge and pointed to the nude body on the couch. 'There are seven more upstairs.'

'*Seven more*?' Flanagan exclaimed, stunned.

'I know it's hard to believe,' Kelly answered. 'You'd better go up, sir, and see for yourself.'

As Flanagan came down the stairs, he shook his head in disbelief. Words had failed him completely.

No time was lost. In less than two hours after the killings had been reported, 140 detectives had been mustered and split up into twenty-man teams deployed to canvass Chicago's South Side to saturation point. They were ordered to check out bars, restaurants, pawnshops, rooming-houses, hotels, motels, gas service depots, second-hand clothing stores. The suspect's description was teletyped to every law enforcement agency throughout the US, Canada and Mexico:

WANTED: White male, 25, 6ft., 170 lbs., short hair, no hat, black waist-length jacket, dark trousers. Stated he wanted money to go to New Orleans. May be armed with revolver and/or knife.

Nine months later, a jury in Peoria, the third largest city in the state of Illinois, took just forty-nine minutes to find Richard Franklin Speck guilty, after an eight-week trial. Peoria was chosen because the defence considered that he would not get a fair trial in Chicago. He was condemned to die in the electric chair, but the US Supreme Court shortly afterwards outlawed capital punishment (reversed in 1976) and Speck's sentence was commuted to a number of consecutive life terms which added up to more than 600 years in prison, which meant in effect that he could never be paroled. His counsel did appeal in 1976, but parole was refused.

In prison, Speck was interviewed and studied in depth by a psychiatrist, Dr. Marvin Ziporyn, who gave it as his opinion that Speck was in an alcohol- and drug-induced psychotic trance on the night of the killings. He was known to have taken various drugs as well as huge quantities of alcohol – an amount, Ziporyn stated, that would have killed a man not used to drinking. Speck may have originally intended only to rob the women, the doctor concludes, until the sight of Gloria Davy triggered a mechanism of violence. It had been discovered that Gloria Davy bore a most remarkable resemblance to the unfaithful wife of his youth.

While Speck had still been living with her, her infidelities had infuriated him to use violence against her and eventually led to the break-up of the marriage. In 1965 – while he was still living with his wife – he had been arrested for assaulting a woman who was parking her car nearby by pressing a carving-knife against her throat. A neighbour had heard her screams, and Speck had run off, but he was quickly caught and sentenced to 490 days in jail. It transpired that this woman, who had been quietly minding her own business and had not provoked Speck in any way, was an almost exact lookalike of his wife – 'she was a dead ringer for my wife,' as Speck told Ziporyn. The doctor considered that this attack, and the attack on Gloria Davy, are too much of a coincidence to be ignored.

Some murders have occurred in areas where Speck was known to be at the material times which have not officially been attributed to him. Dr Ziporyn and others concerned with his case have tried to keep an open mind – Speck himself has denied any involvement in any other murders.

In March 1966 Speck had continuously badgered Mary Pierce, a divorcee who worked in a bar, for a date, but she consistently refused. On 10 April 1966 she disappeared, and three days later her naked body was found in an outbuilding behind the bar where she worked. Speck admitted knowing her, but maintained that he knew nothing about her murder. The record does not reveal whether she had been strangled or stabbed, or both. The case was never officially solved.

Five days later, a sixty-five-year old woman reported that she had been robbed and raped at gunpoint. Her description of her assailant closely approximated the description of

Speck in police records, but when police looked for him in order to question him, he was nowhere to be found. No one was ever charged with this offence.

On 3 May, while working on board ship, he was hospitalized for appendicitis, as mentioned earlier in this account, and made friends with a nurse. He certainly seemed to have a thing about nurses. By June 23, now out of hospital, Speck took this girl swimming and dancing, and also to the movies. She recalls that, 'he had a great deal of repressed hatred within him', and he told her that 'there were two people in Texas he would kill if he had the chance', although he did not say who these people were. It would seem that his wife must have been one of the two persons to whom he had been referring, for he had been reported as having told a friend that he bore his wife a deep grudge, and that 'one day he would go back to Texas and kill her if it was the last thing he ever did.'

On 27 June of the same year Speck obtained a job on a ship, but was dismissed five days later, in Indiana Harbour, for being drunk while on duty. That same day, in nearby Dunes Park, three girls vanished, leaving all their clothes behind them in their car. They had, it seems, been wearing swimwear. Their bodies were never found and when police were investigating their mysterious disappearance, they also learned that there had been another mass murder in Benton Harbour, Michigan, about fifty miles from Indiana Harbour, in February. The victims were all female, their ages ranging from seven to sixty. All had been stabbed to death. It was known that Richard Franklin Speck had arrived in the area at the same time on his way to Monmouth, Illinois.

Dr Marvin Ziporyn thinks that these unsolved crimes, and the presence of Speck in the immediate vicinity at the same time, may be more than pure coincidence. I am inclined to agree with him.

# CHAPTER NINE

## The Monster of Düsseldorf

The Monster of Düsseldorf's reign of terror began at nine o'clock on the evening of 3 February 1929, when a Frau Kühn was accosted by a stranger as she was walking along a street in that city. As she turned to face him he grabbed her and inflicted eighteen stab wounds with almost lightning rapidity to her head, arms and body through her clothing, taking her so completely by surprise that she could not even cry out. This was the first documented crime to be ascribed to Peter Kürten who was to hold the German city in a grip of terror for the next sixteen months until 24 May 1930, when he was arrested at gunpoint by a policeman. The series of crimes which were to be perpetrated by this one man since the night when he greeted Frau Kühn with a quiet *'Guten Abend!'* (Good-evening!) was almost without parallel in criminal history.

Peter Kürten was born in 1883 in Köln-Mulheim, where he spent the first eleven years of his childhood, the family moving to Düsseldorf in 1894. In 1897 he was apprenticed as a moulder. His first known brush with the law followed soon afterwards, in 1899, for a petty theft from a fellow-apprentice.

At this point it is of considerable interest to explore his family history so as to see what light his heredity throws on the subsequent development of his criminal propensities. Peter Kürten was the third of thirteen children. The whole family was well known for its violence and criminality — three of his brothers were habitual thieves and served terms of imprisonment. His father was a confirmed alcoholic, as was his father before him. Peter's father had also served terms of imprisonment for theft and for maintaining an incestuous relationship with one of his daughters. The only light in this background of gloom was his mother, who was a decent, hard-working woman of the working class. His father in his drunken rages used to smash windows and furniture and beat his wife and children, and even in his sexual relations with his wife he would use violence and inflict pain and indignity on her. In the cramped, slum conditions of their home, young Peter frequently witnessed these sexual relations. Later, after his arrest in 1930, he was examined in depth by the eminent psychiatrist, Dr Karl Berg, who expressed the opinion that this may have played a significant part in the development of his sadistic impulses. In his mind sex was fused with cruelty and violence.

The doctor also discovered that a man whom Peter knew in his childhood had initiated him, as a boy, into the torture of animals. This man was a town council employee whose duties were to round up stray dogs and to destroy rats and other vermin. Peter told Dr Berg that he used to enjoy watching the sufferings of dogs, cats and other animals and that the sight of blood excited him sexually. This man also used to accompany his sadistic acts by sexual indignities, which served still further to inflame the boy's erotic sensations, and linked them with the sight of blood, which played a very large part in the sadistic fantasies of his adult life. Dr Berg, who wrote a masterly study of Peter Kürten,* is convinced that this early conditioning played a major part in the formation of the Monster of Düsseldorf's sadistic perversions. Long before Kürten turned to murder, he used to stab sheep, goats and pigs, much to the fury of local farmers, who were never able to catch him, or even know who it was who was attacking their livestock.

After Peter's release from prison in 1899 he returned home to find that his long-suffering mother had divorced

*BERG, Karl. *The Sadist*. (Heinemann, 1933)

his father, unable to cope any longer with his brutalities. Shortly afterwards Peter met a masochistic woman who enjoyed co-operating with him in his sadistic sexual practices. However, they did not live together for very long.

In November of the same year Kürten so abused a girl during sexual intercourse that he left her for dead in the Grafenbergerwald. He proved to himself that his greatest heights of sexual ecstasy could only be attained in this way. Since no body was ever found, it is likely that the victim lived, keeping her horrific experience to herself, and indeed we have only Kürten's statement, revealed to Dr Berg, that this incident ever took place. Kürten referred to it as 'his first murder', although there was no proof that the girl was killed. From that point onwards, however, as the record shows, Peter Kürten was a man prepared to go even to the extent of taking life in order to obtain sexual gratification.

Later the same year he attempted to strangle an eighteen-year-old girl, whose name does not appear in the record, and for this offence he was sentenced to four years in prison. This was but the second of seventeen prison terms he would serve, totalling twenty-seven years out of the forty-seven years he would live from his birth to his execution.

Kürten, while in prison, had so perfected his powers of imagination that he was able to attain orgasm merely by visualizing sadistic fantasies and in order to obtain solitude for indulgences of this kind he committed various minor infractions of prison rules, punishable by solitary confinement. He revealed to Dr Berg that among such fantasies he did not only imagine himself committing atrocities against individuals, but also causing major disasters such as blowing up bridges just as trains were passing over them, handing out arsenic-injected chocolates to whole classes of school children, or introducing deadly bacilli into municipal drinking water, resulting in thousands of deaths by poisoning. He told Dr Berg, 'I derived the same kind of pleasure from this that other men would obtain from thinking about a naked woman.'

It was during this prison sentence too, that he started to

imagine himself causing death by acts of arson. The setting of a fire which quickly built up into a huge conflagration, in which hundreds of people died, was one of his favourite fantasies. On his release in 1904 he decided to put his arson fantasies into practice and he immediately found that, just as he had attained orgasm merely by imagining a fire, the same result followed from setting a fire in reality. Fortunately, however, he did not set any fires resulting in thousands of deaths; he torched such items as hayricks, barns, farm outbuildings and so on, and imagined the deaths of people in the flames.

During his later conversations with the psychiatrist Dr Berg, he admitted the intense pleasure the sight of the flames and the imagined cries for help and screams of the victims had afforded him. This, however, came to light only after his arrest; at the time of the offences the Police certainly had no idea that the acts of arson were sexually motivated, and indeed at that time very little was known about this particular perversion.

In 1905 he was back in prison, having set fire to a barn after harvest, a hay loft and two hayricks. After serving several years he was released, but it was not long before he was arrested once more, this time for abusing a young servant girl named Margrete Schäfer. For this he was re-committed to prison in September 1912. Also taken into account were two further offences, discharging a gun in a public place, to wit, a restaurant, and molesting an unnamed woman in the street. In August 1913 he was released and when he returned home his mother said, in effect, that enough was enough. If he wished to pursue the lifestyle of a criminal she had no place for him in her home. He quickly found lodgings in Köln-Mulheim, and as he was unemployed he supported himself by burglary, at which he was singularly adept – so much so, that he was never apprehended for any of these offences which came to light only during his conversations with Dr Berg after his arrest.

On 25 May 1913 Kürten committed the first of his known

murders. He broke into a tavern and raped the ten-year-old daughter of the proprietor as she lay in bed and then cut her throat. A curious side-effect of this crime was that the victim's uncle was accused of, and tried for, this dreadful deed, but he was acquitted owing to lack of evidence. This man died on active service with the stigma still attached to his name. Naturally Kürten made no attempt to draw the attention of the authorities to this miscarriage of justice . . .

The next thing we know of Kürten's activities is that during the course of a burglary he attacked a girl who was asleep in bed, but something or somebody – it is not clear who or what – frightened him off, and this saved her life.

This is a very interesting instance of the efficient operation of the instinct for self-preservation, even at the same time as the compulsive sex urge was impelling the psychopath to commit yet another sadistic atrocity. Dr Berg ascribes Kürten's long immunity from discovery to his adroitness as a criminal. He was untroubled by remorse and entirely without feeling for his victims. He claimed that he never had nightmares – though the kind of dreams he had, of death, sex and blood, would doubtless have been classed as nightmares had he been normal.

The war years saw Kürten in prison for a number of arson offences, but before his six-year sentence, the year 1913 was not devoid of occasions when he attacked both men and women with an axe or, on one such foray, a pair of scissors. Only one of these victims, a woman named Gertrud Franken, could be identified, because she was the only victim from this particular period to come forward to testify against him at his trial.

One may easily conjecture that had Kürten been at liberty during the war he would have been the first to volunteer as a soldier, with the express aim of getting sent out to the front to fight and thus be able to witness blood and death, even at the risk to his own life. Still, to his way of thinking, being in prison during the war had its compensations: food was being made available for the fighting forces with concomitant cuts in prison rations. Many of the half-starved prisoners died, and Kürten was assiduous in volunteering for the task of laying out the dead. He also stole morphine and other drugs from the prison hospital where he worked as a volunteer male nurse.

In 1921 he was released, and went to Altenburg, where he met the woman who was to become his wife. He spun her a romantic tale about being a war prisoner back from Russia. He had certainly been a prisoner during the war, but not in Russia . . .

The marriage, at least to start with, must have had a stabilizing and restraining effect on him, for under its apparent influence Kürten functioned for well over two years as a normal member of society, pursuing an honest job and becoming active in trade union circles. There were one or two minor lapses, which resulted in charges of ill-treatment of servant girls, but his wife, who was devoted to him, stood loyally by him and the charges were dropped. This two-year period ended in 1925 when Kürten returned to Düsseldorf, having arranged for his wife to follow later when he had obtained a new job and accommodation. 'The sunset was blood-red on my return to Düsseldorf,' he was later to recount to Dr Berg, 'and I considered this to be an omen symbolic of my destiny.' It is conjectured that he had decided to leave Altenburg because he could feel his sadistic urges coming upon him with increasing frequency and needed the anonymity of a great city to cloak his activities. While he had made some effort to control his abnormal propensities, after about two years or so he had come to a point when he realized that he might no longer be able to subdue them. The irksome restrictions of a small town hampered him just at those times when his sadistic compulsions were most dominant in his mind. He was known to have a great partiality for reading about London's Jack the Ripper, which he found very stimulating and re-read the details countless times, but by this time he was now aware that reading and fantasizing alone were insufficient to satisfy him. Now, in the darkness of the

111

city's night streets, he would be able to reach heights of sexual ecstasy which the world of books and his imagination could not encompass.

Although the Monster of Düsseldorf's reign of terror officially began on 3 February 1929 only because the stabbing of Frau Kühn was the first of his victims to come to the notice of the Police, the year 1925 was to herald the commencement of a long series of attacks against persons and property for which he was able to evade suspicion. He attempted, on various dates in that year, to strangle a twenty-four-year-old war widow whose name is undocumented, a young woman named Tiedemann and three young girls named Mech, Kiefer and Waeck. By the time he had committed these outrages it was time for him to think about committing a few acts of arson for good measure. Between 1926 and the beginning of 1929 he committed a total of twenty-six crimes of arson, all except three of which were on farm property and totalling several hundred thousand marks' worth of damage, but no lives were lost. Interspersed between the setting of these fires – one was a forest fire and two left empty houses ablaze – Kürten tried to strangle a young girl whose name is given in the record simply as 'Anni'. No more information is available; her status is given as '*Mädchen*' (young girl) and this description could apply to any female between the ages of thirteen or fourteen and the early twenties.

His next attack was the vicious assault upon Frau Kühn, a twenty-four-year-old married woman, stabbed eighteen times with a pair of scissors on 3 February 1929. From this point onwards Kürten's crimes gained momentum and the Police, although unable to discover their perpetrator, were able to date many of them accurately. Because the killer's *modus operandi* differed occasionally, the Police were not naïve enough to ascribe the murders and other assaults to more than one person. They realized early on that the mark of the madman was indeed able to assume many forms, and that it was criminal cunning that enabled him to vary the nature of his attacks in an attempt to mislead them.

Whatever degree of satisfaction Kürten's attack on Frau Kühn may have afforded him it was obviously not enough for him, since she survived. The next victim, he decided, must die. He chose a man this time, one Rudolf Scheer, a forty-five-year-old businessman, whom he stabbed to death in the street as he was leaving a tavern. As he later told Dr Berg, 'I would have preferred it to be a woman, but no woman was available at the time.' The date was 13 February, only ten days after the stabbing of Frau Kühn.

On 8 March Kürten strangled a child named Rose Ohliger. She was eight years old and he stabbed her dead body eighteen times and raped her after death. He then buried her in a shallow grave in a wooded area. However, his necrophilic blood-lust was seemingly still not sated, for not long after he had committed this atrocity, he attempted to strangle a young girl named Edith Boukorn. Fortunately she managed to escape with her life. In July he made three more attempts to strangle young women, Maria Witt, Maria Mass, and another whose name is not recorded. It seemed only a matter of time now before he would succeed in killing again.

Time was to prove him right. In August he strangled a young woman named Maria Hahn and stabbed her twenty times after death. However, her fate was not known until 14 November, when her brutalized body was found. In August, when she disappeared, she had been reported only as missing. In his confessions to Dr Berg, Kürten said of this murder, 'I caressed the dead body as it lay in the grave, experiencing the tenderest emotions that as a living woman she had failed to arouse in me earlier . . .' The following day he returned to the woodland grave, bringing with him some metal spikes, with the intention of crucifying the corpse. He abandoned this intention, however, when he found, on disinterring it, that the inert body was too heavy for him to lift. Kürten also visited a cemetery in which the body of the child he had killed in 1913 was buried. Seating himself upon the grave, he fingered the earth and drifted into a macabre reverie, during which orgasm occurred. 'It was the fantasy of loving a dead being,' he told Berg.

We are indebted to Dr Karl Berg for this insight into the mind of a multiple murderer, for it is indeed only very rarely that such a killer will reveal the details of his crimes and his feelings when committing them. Albert DeSalvo, the Boston Strangler, was another such mass murderer who unburdened himself to a psychiatrist. But Peter Kürten was undoubtedly the one who gave the most exact and complete description of his crimes including the large number which were never reported by those victims who survived, as well as those where victims died but were never discovered by the Police. In many cases, indeed, the Police had no proof, and relied on the murderer's own confession coupled with circumstantial evidence.

Quite unsuspected by his wife, his friends, his neighbours or the authorities, Kürten continued his terrifying orgy of crime unchallenged and unmolested for another ten months until his nemesis finally caught up with him. Still, in August 1929, after killing Maria Hahn, he strangled a girl recorded merely as 'Anni' and drowned her in the Rhine. On 21 August he stabbed with a dagger sixteen-year-old Anna Goldhausen, a young woman named Frau Mantel, thirty years old, and a man, Gustav Kornblum. All these three escaped. Questioned by police as their wounds were stitched in hospital, they all said that it had been dark at the time and they could not see their assailant's face nor, since he did not speak, describe his voice. The Police were stymied. Each time the attacker struck, he vanished into the darkness quickly and silently.

24 August was to see Kürten's frenzy reach a peak. In one day, he strangled and stabbed a fourteen-year-old girl names Luise Lenzen, strangled and cut the throat of a five-year-old child named Gertrud Hamacher, and stabbed a twenty-six-year-old woman named Gertrud Schulte with a dagger, leaving her lying bleeding but still alive. Again, this victim was unable to give police any useful lead. So the Monster of Düsseldorf was still free to carry on his dreadful work. Later that same month he attacked a girl named

Christina Heerstrasse, strangled her and threw her body into the River Düssel.

September dawned, and a young woman named Sofia Rueckl was walking home from work when she was hit on the head with a hammer. She survived. Another young woman, Maria Rad, was the victim of an attempted strangulation, but managed to fight off her assailant and flee screaming. Police called to the public gardens where she had been attacked found them deserted. These two attempts, however, did not satisfy Kürten; his next victim, Ida Reuter, was bludgeoned to death with a hammer. The hammer was used in his next three attacks in October 1929. The first victim, a young woman named Elisabeth Dorrier, died from her injuries, but the other two survived. Frau Meurer, a married woman of thirty-four, and Frau Wanders, whose age is not recorded, were again unable to describe their attacker.

On 7 November 1929 the body of a five-year-old-girl, Gertrud Albermann, was found strangled. She had been stabbed with scissors after death thirty-six times and raped. This is the last known murder attributed to Peter Kürten. His subsequent assaults, which included attempted strangulation and attacks with a hammer, did not result in death. In several cases, the girls' names are recorded only as 'Hilda' (February 1930), 'Maria' and 'Irma B., aged 22' (March 1930), 'Sybilla', 'an unknown girl', and 'a young woman surnamed Hau', 'several young girls' and one Charlotte Ulrich, all in April 1930.

Four earlier cases were attributed to Kürten only later at his trial. These were the attempted strangulation of Erna Pinner, aged sixteen, on 2 April 1929; the attempted strangulation of Frau Flake on 3 April 1919; the strangling on 30 July 1929 of a thirty-five-year-old prostitute named Emma Gross, and a hammer attack on an unnamed young woman on 30 March 1930.

Time was now running out for this unspeakable pervert who had held a huge city in the grip of terror for more than a year. The murders were headlined in every newspaper in the civilized world; 9,000 people had been interrogated in Düsseldorf alone and the files on the case at police headquarters were indexed on 70,000 cards. Even as far away as Budapest a man was arrested after muttering something about 'Düsseldorf' to a nervous girl friend. Yet this man, who was forty-seven at the time of his arrest but looked little more than thirty, was the very last person anyone suspected as being the perpetrator of these monstrous crimes. He was soft-voiced, well-spoken and always well-groomed from head to toe – he even carried a shoe-polishing cloth in his coat pocket. His manners were impeccable, and he was very attractive to women, which may account for the ease with which he was able to get into conversation with complete strangers. One young girl who testified at his trial admitted that although he had twice tried to throttle her during the course of one evening when she had gone out with him, she still arranged to meet him again later, and said, 'I could not sleep that night for thinking of him . . .' Fortunately for her, the 'date' they had arranged was after his arrest.

Children, too, seemed to be attracted to him, and many witnesses said that they seemed to trust him instinctively. In his normal moments, he appeared to love children, who would run to him, and he would pat them on the head and play games with them. In fact many people would not believe that Peter Kürten, when arrested, could possibly be the 'Düsseldorf Monster'. The girl who had made the date to meet him later, said in court, 'He cannot possibly be the Düsseldorf murderer. The police are making a mistake in the man's identity.'

This sadistic murderer and pyromaniac lived quietly with his wife and never once to anyone's knowledge lifted a hand against her. He was devoted to her, after his fashion. They had no children, and heredity being what it is, this was perhaps a good thing. Frau Kürten never had any reason to suspect that her husband was anything other than the gentle and helpful man he was at home. He always ate and slept well, seemingly untroubled by his *alter ego*. Frau

116

Kürten worked in a restaurant until after midnight, and was just as terrified as all her neighbours of the Düsseldorf Monster. Her husband used to accompany her to her work, and call for her at 12.30 a.m. to bring her safely home to their flat at 71 Mettmännerstrasse.

Despite the unceasing efforts of all the best police brains in the whole of Germany, the German Police can claim no credit for the arrest of the Monster, which was the result of pure chance.

In May 1930, an unemployed twenty-year-old girl named Maria Budlik took a train to Düsseldorf from her home village in response to an offer of work as a housemaid from a Frau Brugmann, who lived in the city. They had arranged to meet at Düsseldorf railway station on the evening in question, but Maria's prospective employer did not turn up to keep the appointment. Maria inquired of a passing man the way to a hostel for girls and he offered to escort her there. When he started to lead her into the park, however, she became nervous and refused to go with him any further. While the argument was taking place, another man approached, having heard Maria's appeal for help, and drove the first man off. The girl gratefully accepted the offer of a coffee from the quiet stranger, who had saved her from 'a fate worse than death' and who was, unknown to her, Peter Kürten.

He took her back to his flat, where they had coffee and sandwiches, after which he said he would escort her to the girls' hostel. On the way he led her through a wooded area, where he started to throttle her. Then, just as suddenly, he released her, with no explanation, saying, 'Do you remember where I live, just in case you ever need my help again?' Maria did some very quick thinking. Not anticipating needing his help, she told him a lie, which undoubtedly saved her life, but cost Kürten his own. She told him that she could not remember his address, after which Kürten accompanied her to a tram stop, saw her on the tram which would take her to the girls' hostel, and went on his way.

Maria Budlik, once installed in the hostel, sat down and wrote a letter to Frau Brugmann, not only inquiring about the job and the abortive appointment, but also relating her experience with the stranger, somewhat facetiously. But this letter was mis-delivered by the postman, who took it to another Frau Brugmann at a different address, who had never heard of Maria Budlik. Mystified by this glimpse of Düsseldorf after dark, she remembered the almost daily headlines in the newspapers, and became even more intrigued by the revelations of this unknown girl. She promptly handed the letter to the Police, who quickly located Maria Budlik at the hostel. She could not remember the number of Kürten's flat but she took detectives to the building in the Mettmännerstrasse and described Kürten to one of the other tenants, who recognized the description. The Monster of Düsseldorf was doomed.

Kürten was actually on the staircase at a lower level when he spotted Maria talking to the detectives and the neighbour. He fled, wandered about all night, and the next morning he rented a room in an adjoining street, where he had a long sleep. Even then, when he knew that the Police were practically on his doorstep, he could still sleep soundly and enjoy his meals. He returned to his wife, whom the Police had interviewed in the meantime and confessed to her that he was indeed the Düsseldorf murderer. He took her out for a meal, but she was too horrified to eat, after he had finally convinced her that he was telling the truth. At first she had refused to believe him, thinking it was just one of his jokes. She left her food untouched, and after he had finished his own meal, he then enjoyed hers. He then told her that she could tell the Police that he had confessed to her, so that she could claim a reward which had been offered for his capture. 'It was not easy to convince her that this would not be betraying me,' he told Berg.

After this remarkable performance, he then returned to his rented room, where the Police could not find him, and had another long, sound sleep. He then went out for a walk. It was 24 May 1930. As he was standing outside the Rochus

Church, a policeman, recognizing him from his description which had been circulated to all police stations, drew his revolver and challenged him. Kürten surrendered quietly without a word.

Peter Kürten's trial commenced on 13 April 1931 and lasted ten days. His full confession included more than seventy crimes with which the Police would not otherwise have connected him, and some of this material was included in the depositions, although he was actually indicted for ten specimen charges of murder only. The jury was out for only an hour and a half before finding him guilty on nine charges, and he was sentenced to death. He remained calm and well-behaved while in prison and on the night before his execution he wrote letters of condolence to the relatives of thirteen of his victims.

For his last meal he ordered *wiener schnitzel* with fried potatoes and white wine, which he enjoyed so much that he asked for a second helping. Then he went quietly to his death by guillotine in Klingelgratz Prison in Köln at 6 a.m. on 2 July 1931. His last words were to ask the headsman whether for a fleeting moment he would be able to hear the gushing of his own blood as his head was severed from his body.

# CHAPTER TEN

## Son of Sam

After the catalogue of atrocities committed by Peter Kürten, it is almost a relief to turn to a killer who could count the number of victims on his fingers. Such a killer was David Berkowitz, who came to be known as the 'Son of Sam'.

On the night of 29 July 1976 two young girls were sitting in the front seats of a car parked on Buhre Avenue, in New York City. They were Donna Lauria, a medical technician, and Jody Valenti, a student nurse. Donna's parents, on their way home from a night out in the city, passed them as they sat in their car at about 1 a.m., and greeted them with a cheery 'Good-night!' A few moments after they reached their apartment, which was not far away, they heard the sounds of shots and screams. A man had walked up to the parked Oldsmobile car, pulled a gun out of a brown paper bag, and fired five shots. Donna was killed instantly, but Jody was only wounded in the thigh.

The total lack of motive for the shooting convinced police that they were dealing with a psychopath who killed merely for the pleasure of killing, choosing random victims he had never seen before. There was no attempt at either robbery or sexual assault. In police parlance, the killer was 'a nutter'.

Their theory appeared to be borne out when, four months later, on 26 November 1976, two young girls were sitting talking on the stoop in front of a house in the Floral Park section of Queens, New York. It was 12.30 a.m. when a man walked up to them, started to ask them directions, and then, even before he had completed the sentence, pulled a gun and began shooting. Another Donna, this time surnamed DeMasi, and Joanne Lomino, were both wounded. A bullet lodged in Joanne's spine, paralysing her for life. The other girl recovered. Bullets dug out of the front door and a mailbox revealed that both girls had been shot by the same .44 that had been used on the previous two victims in July.

Although the police were as yet unaware of it, the same gun had already wounded another victim. Over a month earlier, on 23 October 1976, Carl Denaro and his girl friend Rosemary Keenan were sitting talking in his sports car, parked in front of a tavern in Flushing, New York, when there were several loud bangs and a bullet ripped through the rear windshield, and Carl Denaro fell forward. He was rushed to hospital. In three weeks he was well on the way to recovery, although his middle finger – the report does not specify which hand – was permanently damaged. A .44 bullet was found on the floor of the car.

On 30 January 1977 a young couple were kissing good-night in a car in the Ridgewood area of New York. Suddenly there was a deafening explosion, the windshield shattered, and Christine Freund slumped into the arms of her boy friend, John Diel. She died a few hours later in hospital.

On 8 March 1977 Virginia Voskerichian, an Armenian student, was on her way home, only a few hundred yards from her mother's house in Forest Hills, New York, when a gunman walked up to her and calmly shot her in the face at only a few yards' range. The bullet went into her mouth, shattering her front teeth. She died immediately.

By now the police had discovered that all the bullets which had killed three and wounded four had come from the same gun. This indicated a homicidal psychopath who would most likely continue shooting at random until he was caught. The problem was that the Police had no clues whatsoever to his identity, and no idea of where to begin looking. The shootings had happened so fast, and the assailant had disappeared afterwards so quickly, that no one had any description to offer. Unless he were actually caught during an attempt on someone else's life, any chance of arresting him seemed remote. He always struck under cover of darkness, which gave him the advantage of being able to melt into the shadows.

Mayor Beame of New York held a Press conference, during which he announced, 'We have a savage killer on the loose.' He was able to say only that the man was white, approximately five feet ten inches tall, well-groomed, and wore his hair combed straight back.

On the morning of 17 April 1977 there were two more deaths. The victims were Alexander Esau and Valentina Suriani who had been sitting in their parked car in the Bronx when the killer shot them both. Valentina was killed instantly; Esau died a few hours later in hospital, with three bullets in his head. These killings occurred only a few blocks away from where Donna Lauria and Jody Valenti had been shot.

In the middle of the street, a policeman found an envelope containing a letter addressed to Captain Joseph Borelli of the New York Police. It transpired that this letter had been written by the killer. 'I am deeply hurt by your calling me a woman-hater,' he had written, 'I am not. But I am a monster. I am the Son of Sam.' The letter went on to claim that his father, Sam, was a brute who had abused his family when he was drunk, and who ordered his son to go out and kill. It was rather reminiscent of the letters that Jack the Ripper and some other killers had written to the Police, as though by getting into the headlines it would satisfy their urge to 'be somebody', to make an impact on society.

A further rambling, incoherent note, signed 'Son of Sam', was sent to a New York journalist, James Breslin. But Breslin decided not to pander to the deranged killer's compulsive lust for publicity; instead he handed the letter to the Police.

The next attack, which took place on 26 June 1977, closely resembled previous attacks. A young couple sitting in their car in the early hours of Sunday morning, saying good-night after a date, were shot at almost point-blank range. The couple, Salvatore Lupo and Judy Placido, were parked in front of a house in 211th Street in the Bayside area of Queens. The windshield shattered as four shots were fired and the assailant fled. Fortunately for the young couple, his aim had been poor, and they were only wounded.

It was now a year since the Son of Sam had killed Donna Lauria. On 29 July, the anniversary of her death, Queens and the Bronx were swarming with police, but the Son of Sam had decided that these areas were too risky and that his next shootings should take place as far away as possible. On 31 July Robert Violante and Stacy Moskowitz were sitting in their parked car in a parking lot close to the Brooklyn beach. It was 1.30 a.m. on a Sunday morning – seemingly a favourite time and day for the Son of Sam to choose for his attacks. The windshield exploded as four shots were fired without any warning. Both were hit in the head. Stacy Moskowitz died hours later in hospital; Robert Violante recovered, but was blinded for life. This shooting, however, was the one that provided the break in the case.

A woman out walking her dog had noticed two policemen attaching a parking ticket to a car parked near a fire hydrant on Bay 16th Street. Moments later, a man ran up to the car, leapt in and drove off at speed. Only four parking tickets had been issued in the Bay area that Sunday morning, and only one of those was for parking near a hydrant, which is illegal. The carbon copy of the ticket in the policeman's notebook contained the registration number of the car, and the Vehicle Licensing Department was able to identify its owner as one David Berkowitz, aged twenty-four, of Pine Street, Yonkers.

On the Wednesday after the last killing, detectives found a Ford Galaxie parked in front of an apartment building in Pine Street. Peering in through its window, the officers noticed the butt of a gun, and also a note, written in block capitals and similar in appearance to the other 'Son of Sam' letters. The car was staked out, and when David Berkowitz approached it at 10.15 that evening, Deputy Inspector Tim Dowd, who had led the hunt, said to him, 'Hello, David.'

Berkowitz looked at him in surprise, then replied, 'Inspector Dowd! You finally got me!'

After all the terror he had aroused, the arrest of the Son of Sam was something of an anticlimax. He was a pudgy little man with a beaming smile and a tendency to look like a slightly simple-minded child who had been caught stealing cookies from the kitchen jar. He was a paranoid schizophrenic, a man who lived alone in a room lit only by a naked bulb and slept on a bare mattress. The floor was littered with empty milk cartons and bottles. On the walls he had scrawled messages such as, 'In this hole lives the Wicked King', 'I kill for my Master' and 'I turn children into killers'.

His father, who had run a hardware store in the Bronx, had left the area after his shop was burgled and moved to Florida. Nat Berkowitz was not in fact David's real father. David, who was born on 1 June 1953, had been illegitimate, and his mother had offered him for adoption. He had felt rejected right from birth. He reacted to his poor self-image by boasting and lying, particularly about his sexual prowess. In fact he was shy, avoided women, and was almost certainly a virgin.

He told police that 'demons' began telling him to kill as far back as 1974, although one of the psychiatrists who interviewed him is convinced that this is not true. 'Berkowitz's stories of voices,' he said, 'were merely an attempt to establish a defence of insanity.' Living alone in rooms that he allowed to become pigsties, kept awake at night by the sound of rumbling trucks or barking dogs, he slipped into paranoia. In a letter to his father he said that people hated him and spat at him as he walked along the street. 'Girls call me ugly,' he wrote, 'and they bother me the most.'

It was on Christmas Eve, 1975, that David Berkowitz began his campaign of revenge against women, by taking a knife and attacking two girls. The first one screamed so loudly that he ran away; the second, a fifteen-year-old schoolgirl, was badly cut, and sustained a punctured lung.

Seven months later, Berkowitz went out with a gun and committed his first murder.

The name 'Sam' seems to have been borrowed from a neighbour called Sam Carr. This man kept a black Labrador dog, whose barking frequently kept Berkowitz awake. He wrote Carr anonymous letters and on 27 April 1977 shot the dog, but not fatally. He also wrote anonymous letters to people he believed to be persecuting him. He had been reported to the Police on a number of occasions as 'a nutcase', but no one suspected that he might be the 'Son of Sam'.

Berkowitz was adjudged sane at his arraignment on 23 August 1977 and pleaded guilty, saving New York the cost of a lengthy trial. He was sentenced to 365 years in prison, which may sound ludicrous to those not familiar with the American system of criminal law. The number of years is arrived at by adding together life terms when there are several indictments, in order to ensure that a dangerous homicidal maniac cannot ever be granted parole.

The aftermath is worth mentioning. The Yonkers apartment block where Berkowitz had his last room became a place of pilgrimage for sensation-seekers, who stole doorknobs, cut out pieces of the carpet, unscrewed fittings, even chipped pieces of paint from the door. In the middle of the night people would shout, 'David, come out!' from the street. Berkowitz's room remained vacant, and more than a quarter of the building's other tenants moved out. The landlord even changed the building's number from 25 to 42 in an effort to mislead the souvenir hunters. The record does not state how the postal authorities reacted to this futile move.

# CHAPTER ELEVEN

## The Vampire of Montreal

On 23 July 1968 a twenty-one-year-old teacher named Norma Vaillancourt was found in her Montreal apartment raped and strangled. Her breasts were covered with human bite marks. Oddly enough, according to the forensic pathologist's report, there was no sign that the victim had put up even a token resistance. Even the expression on her face was serene, the pathologist noted. Norma had been a popular girl and had many boy friends, all of whom were eliminated from the investigation.

In 1969 the body of Shirley Audette was found on a patio at the rear of an apartment complex in West Montreal. Although her body was fully clothed, it transpired that she had been raped and strangled. There were thirty-nine human bite marks on her breasts. Once more police were confident that Shirley had known her killer, for there were no signs whatsoever of violent resistance. There was no skin or flesh under the fingernails, not a single bruise on the body. It seemed clear that she had felt no harm would come to her . . .

On further investigation, however, police elicited some disturbing information from one of her friends. Shirley had told her, with some reluctance, that she thought she was 'getting into something dangerous with a new boy friend'. They also found that her regular boy friend was very worried about her. He told them that Shirley had telephoned him at 3 a.m. on the day she died and told him, 'I'm scared!' but had not elaborated. The most obvious explanation, police surmised, seemed to be that Shirley had become involved with a man who, although outwardly charming, had strange inclinations. Possibly, he chose girls whom he intinctively felt had at least some masochistic leanings. Such girls would submit to a certain degree of biting and mock strangling during the course of a sexual relationship, but he got carried away, with fatal results. Many men (though not all) who have sadistic tendencies during sexual intercourse have no intention of actually killing, but it is all too easily accomplished. Some of these men, of course, do have homicidal intent, for them the act of killing provides a sexual thrill. The Montreal Police, however, had no way of knowing which category the unknown killer belonged to.

The next killing confirmed that he was not, at any rate, a rapist who chose his victims at random. On 23 November 1969 a clerk at a jewellery store named Marielle Archambault greeted a well-dressed young man as 'Bill'. Fellow-workers gained the impression that she was pleased, even excited, to see him. It was not quite closing time, and 'Bill' waited for her outside the store. They then left together.

When Marielle failed to arrive for work next morning and did not telephone in sick, her employer became concerned. It was unlike Marielle to be late, or not to let him know if she could not report for work for any reason. She was one of the most reliable employees they had. He decided to call her landlady who went to see whether the girl was ill. Getting no response to her knock, she found the door to Marielle's flat unlocked. She went in and found the girl's body on the living-room floor, naked but partly covered with a blanket. There were signs of a fierce struggle, which had ended in her death. The killer had removed her tights and raped her, and torn off her brassière in order to cover her breasts with bites.

The Police, when conducting a search of the apartment, found the crumpled photograph of a young man. When shown to the dead girl's fellow-workers at the jewellery store, they immediately identified it as the same young man

127

who had called for her the previous afternoon. A sketch was made up from this photograph and published in all the Montreal papers, alongside the screaming headlines of the more sensational journals: 'A Vampire is Loose in Montreal!' and the like. No one, however, came forward to identify the 'Vampire Killer'.

Two months later, a twenty-four-year-old secretary named Jean Way had arranged a date with her boy friend for 16 January 1970. When he knocked on the door of her Montreal apartment at the pre-arranged time of 8.15 p.m., there was no reply. He assumed that she had, perhaps, gone out briefly to fetch a newspaper, or perhaps was taking a shower and could not hear a knock. He decided to go and have a beer in a nearby bar, and return later. When he did so, he saw that the door was slightly ajar. Still he was not alarmed, as he assumed that Jean had left the door open for him while she was occupied – perhaps telephoning her widowed mother, or something of that kind. He entered the flat. He found Jean lying on the living-room sofa, totally nude, her breasts bearing mute and bloody evidence of the hallmark of the Vampire Killer.

On the evidence, it seemed likely, police thought, that her killer had actually been with her at the time when the boy friend knocked on the first occasion. There was no sign of a struggle or any disarray in the room. Her face, according to the forensic pathologist who conducted the autopsy, looked 'composed in death'.

Despite immense publicity and massive police activity, Canada's most wanted murderer remained at large, but the 'Vampire Killer of Montreal' decided that his home territory was becoming a little too crowded for safety. His next killing took place 2,500 miles away in Calgary, Alberta. A young schoolteacher, Elizabeth Anne Porteous, had failed to arrive on the morning of 18 May 1971, and as the morning wore on with no word from her, a member of the staff was sent from the school to call at her home and inquire whether she was ill. When repeated knocking on her door elicited no reply, the school staff member contacted the apartment house manager who fetched a duplicate key and entered. To his horror, he found Elizabeth's body on the floor of her apartment. She had been raped and strangled, her brassière torn open and her breasts hideously mutilated by the Vampire Killer's frenzied bites. A man's broken cuff-link was found underneath the body.

On the previous evening two fellow-teachers had seen Elizabeth Porteous in a car with a young man. The teachers had pulled up at a traffic light when a blue Mercedes-Benz drew alongside, and they recognized their colleague. The only thing they could remember about the car, apart from its colour and make, was a distinctive sticker of some kind on the rear window as it drove off. They could not give a description of the driver, except to say that he looked young, because they had been concentrating on the lights and the traffic. They had not taken much notice of who was in the car apart from the brief recognition of their colleague.

A colleague who was also a personal friend of the victim was able to tell police that Elizabeth had told her that she had been dating a new boy friend whose name she said was Bill for the past week or so. She had described him as a 'sharp dresser', with a neatly-trimmed hairstyle. This description was also applicable to the man known as 'Bill' who had been seen by the co-workers of the jewellery store clerk in Montreal.

The following day a police officer saw a blue Mercedes-Benz not far from the victim's apartment, and half an hour later a young man was arrested as he approached the car. Like the Son of Sam, who was arrested in exactly similar fashion as he approached his car, he put up no resistance and quietly accompanied the police officers to their vehicle.

He was Wayne Clifford Boden, formerly of Montreal, who had moved to Calgary a year previously. He agreed that he had been with Elizabeth Porteous in her apartment the previous evening and that the cuff-link belonged to him. But he insisted that she had been alive and well when he had left her in her apartment. He was indisputably the man shown in the crumpled photograph which had been found in Marielle Archambault's apartment. The clinching evidence, however, came from an orthodontist who identified the teeth marks on Elizabeth Porteous's breasts as having 29 points of similarity with Boden's dental impressions. In addition, examination by forensic scientists of Boden's underwear had shown seminal stains as well as pubic hairs from the body of Elizabeth Porteous.

Boden was sentenced to life imprisonment for the murder of Elizabeth Porteous; later he was taken to Montreal, to stand trial for the murders committed there. He admitted three of the four killings which had been attributed to him there but he denied that he was the killer of the first victim, Norma Vaillancourt. He was given three more life sentences for the other three rape-stranglings. Four life sentences excluded the possibility of parole.

In retrospect, it seems almost certain that the killings had not been premeditated. Wayne Boden was himself a victim – he was subject to an overwhelming, sadistic obsession with female breasts which, when it got out of hand, carried him along to its inevitable conclusion. It seems more than probable that he succeeded in persuading these unfortunate women that a certain amount of biting and mock strangling was acceptable during lovemaking – though lust rather than love seemed to motivate him in these frenzied attacks. This is the most likely reason why all but one of his victims lost consciousness and died without a struggle.

It is to be hoped that Boden is receiving psychiatric treatment in prison. Although he will never again be allowed to become a menace to women in the outside world, such treatment would go at least some way to relieve the intensity of his dreadful compulsions – and maybe even allow him some insight into their possible cause.

# CHAPTER TWELVE

## The Hillside Strangler

Women and girls began to disappear at an alarming rate in the Seattle area during the first half of 1974. The district, and in fact the whole of Washington state, had never known anything like it.

It all started when Lynda Ann Healy, a student at the University of Washington, suddenly and unaccountably vanished from her rented room on 31 January 1974. Her bedsheets were bloodstained, and so was the nightdress hanging in her closet. Her friends feared the worst, and reported her missing to the Police. From the amount of blood, crime was suspected, but no one had seen or heard anything suspicious. The girl had seemingly vanished into thin air. Intensive inquiries did not turn up a single clue.

Four weeks earlier, a young girl named Sharon Clarke had been attacked as she lay in bed in a house only a few blocks away. The intruder had hit her on the head with a heavy iron rod. She recovered, despite multiple skull fractures, but could remember nothing about the intruder. Police were not sure at first whether to link the two incidents or not. But there were certainly some similarities: the assailant had broken into the girls' rooms, and some injury had been inflicted in both cases.

On 12 March 1974 Donna Gail Manson, a student at Evergreen State College in Olympia, Washington, vanished without trace while on her way to a concert. Five weeks later on 17 April, Susan Rancourt, a student at Washington Central State College in Ellensburg, disappeared on her way to see a German language film. On 6 May Roberta Kathleen Parks, a student at Oregon State University in Corvallis, went out for a late night walk and never returned.

Brenda Ball, a young office worker, was the next girl to vanish without trace after leaving the Flame Tavern, near Seattle Airport, with a man at 2 a.m. on 1 June. Ten days later, on 11 June, Georgianne Hawkins, a student at the University of Washington, left her boy friend on her way back to her sorority house after a date, and was never seen again alive.

On 14 July Doris Grayling was sitting at a picnic table beside Lake Samanish, Washington, when a good-looking young man with his arm in a sling came up and asked her whether she could lend him a hand to lift a boat on to his car. She accompanied him to his Volkswagen, which stood in the car park, but when he said that the boat was at a house up the hill, she made an excuse and left. He smiled pleasantly and apologized for troubling her. A few minutes later she saw him walking past with a blonde girl. Her name was Janice Ott, and some passers-by who happened to overhear the young man introduce himself to the blonde as 'Ted' later described how he had asked her to help him load a sailing boat on to the roof of his car. Janice Ott was never seen alive again.

A few hours later Denise Naslund, another young girl who was enjoying the lakeside amenities on her day off from work, walked into the public toilets and vanished. Other young women who had been approached that day by the personable young man with his arm in a sling who had the problem of getting his boat on to his car, had politely refused. This had undoubtedly saved their lives.

On 7 September 1974 two men out grouse-hunting on a hillside in rural Washington discovered human bodies. The area was a few miles from Lake Samanish. The bodies were badly decomposed and the bones had been scattered by wild animals. After two fragmented skeletons had been reassembled as far as possible, they were later identified as the remains of Janice Ott and

Denise Naslund. A third partial skeleton was too fragmented to be identified.

The stories of 'Ted' brought in a number of reports. A woman in Ellensburg recalled seeing a young man with his arm in a sling on the night Susan Rancourt disappeared. A girl said that a man with his arm in a sling tried to pick her up in downtown Seattle, and when she declined took his arm out of the sling and drove off at speed. Another girl said that a brown Volkswagen had driven up on to the sidewalk close to her, and she had run away.

On 12 October 1974 a hunter in Clark County found a human skull with hair still intact at a spot about 130 miles north of the place of the previous findings. Police subsequently found the remains of two young women in the same remote hillside area. One was identified as Carol Balenzuela of Vancouver, Washington, who had vanished two months earlier. The other body remained unidentified.

Police soon had two possible suspects. A man named Warren Forrest had picked up a woman in Portland, Oregon, persuaded her to pose for some photographs in the park, and then tied her ankles and bound her mouth with tape. He was a municipal employee who worked in the park. He took her to a secluded part of the park, stripped her and then fired darts into her breasts from a pellet-gun. He then assaulted her with a dildo, raped her, and finally strangled her, leaving her for dead. She recovered consciousness and crawled away, and later identified Forrest, who was known to his friends as 'a quiet, normal type'.

When Vonnie Stuth vanished from her home on 27 November 1974, her sister was able to tell police that a neighbour had knocked at her door while she was speaking to her on the telephone, and had apparently asked Vonnie whether she would look after his dog while he moved house. The neighbour, Gary Taylor, proved to be an ex-con with a long record of sexual assaults. Taylor himself as well as Vonnie had vanished when police went looking for him.

The strange disappearances of women and girls had now spread beyond the Seattle area and were causing alarm among the citizens of Salt Lake City, Utah. On 2 October 1974 Nancy Wilcox vanished; on 18 October Melissa Smith, the daughter of a police officer, went to an all-night party, then changed her mind about staying as she did not like the atmosphere. Many of the young people were taking drugs and she set out to walk home. She never arrived. Her raped and strangled body was found nine days later in the Wassatch Mountains, east of Salt Lake City.

On 31 October Laura Aime, a six-foot-tall girl who had a passion for horseriding, set out from a Hallowe'en party after midnight, and never returned home.

On 8 November the Salt Lake City Police had their first break in the case. Carol DaRonch was in a shopping mall when she was approached by a well-dressed young man, who asked her in an official-sounding manner the number of her car. When she told him, he told her that he was a police officer and that there had been an attempt to break into her car. Obediently she went with him to inspect it. The car proved to be still locked. She then allowed herself to be persuaded to go with him 'to view a suspect' at police headquarters. Once in his Volkswagen, he drove to a quiet street, stopped the car and snapped handcuffs on her wrists. When she screamed, he pointed a gun at her head. She managed to lunge out of the car, and grabbed the crowbar he tried to bring down on her head. She ran into the path of an oncoming car, which screeched to a halt. She hurled herself bodily into the car and was driven off by the married couple who were in it. They took her to the Police to file a complaint about the attempted abduction.

That same evening, a good-looking young man tried to pick up a young French teacher outside the Viewmont High School, but she managed to give him the slip. A young student at the school, Deborah Kent, vanished as she left to meet her brother nearby. In the school grounds police found a handcuff key.

On 27 November the naked body of Laura Aime was found in dense undergrowth in a canyon in the Utah desert. But still the Police were no nearer to solving the puzzle of the disappearing women which was plaguing all the law enforcement agencies of two states, and was also to include a third.

On 12 January 1975, a cardiology seminar was beginning in the village of Snowmass, a ski resort in Colorado. A doctor named Raymond Gadowsky was attending the seminar with his fiancée, Caryn Campbell. She vanished from her room at the Wildwood Inn some time during the evening of that first day. Her frozen, nude body was discovered not far away on 17 February. She had been raped and beaten to death.

On 15 March Julie Cunningham, a pretty clerk, set out to meet a girl friend in a bar at Vail, Colorado. The girl friend was left waiting for Julie, who never arrived . . .

Back in Washington, the remains of two more missing girls had been found on Taylor Mountain. From dental evidence, the skulls were identified as those of Brenda Ball and Susan Rancourt, two of the victims from early 1974.

On 15 April Melanie Cooley vanished in Nederland, Colorado. Her body was found eight days later on 23 April on a hillside fifteen miles away. Unlike the other victims she was fully-clothed except for her jeans, which had been pulled down to her ankles. She had been battered to death with a rock.

On 1 July Shelley Roberton disappeared from Golden, Colorado, and her naked body was discovered in a mine near the Berthoud Pass on 23 August.

The Fourth of July meant Independence Day celebrations for most Americans, but there was no celebration for Nancy Baird, a gas depot attendant, who vanished that day from her place of work at Bountiful, Colorado. Her body was never found . . .

In the early hours of the morning of 16 August, a police patrolman on the lookout for possible burglars became suspicious of a Volkswagen in Salt Lake City, Utah, whose driver appeared to be avoiding him. The patrolman eventually blocked off his retreat in an abandoned gas depot. The officer found in the car a ski mask, an ice-pick, a crowbar and other tools which could be used in a burglary. The driver was one Theodore (known as 'Ted') Bundy. The patrolman brought him to headquarters for questioning in connection with suspected burglary.

A police check on Bundy revealed that he was a psychology student from Seattle, who had worked for the Governor's campaign committee. He said that he was in Salt Lake City to study law. A search of Bundy's room revealed nothing suspicious, but maps of various areas of Colorado, including the area near Bountiful, reminded the Police that there had been a number of unsolved disappearances and murders in that state. When hairs found in Bundy's car were found to be identical to those of Melissa Smith, and a witness reported seeing Bundy at the ski lodge in Snowmass on the night Caryn Campbell vanished, he was charged with murder.

In January 1977 he was extradited to Colorado. Bundy became a popular prisoner – his intelligence and good looks made it seem somehow unlikely that he could possibly be a multiple sex killer. He had a lively sense of humour, and acted as his own lawyer. He studied law books and was allowed to have special health foods sent in to the prison for him. The guards also allowed him to make his court appearances without manacles.

The picture of Bundy which witnesses began to build up was unflattering. It showed a liar, a smooth talker, a man who always wanted his own way – in short, something of a con man, yet hardly the type who could be imagined committing sex murders every week or so. The evidence against him, however, piled up relentlessly, and was damning. Carol DaRonch had, albeit hesitantly, identified him as the man who had tried to abduct her and his credit card receipts showed that he had at the appropriate times been close to the places where Caryn Campbell and Julie Cunningham had vanished.

On the morning of 7 June 1977 Ted Bundy opened a window of the Law Library in Aspen, Colorado, and dropped thirty feet to the ground. This daring escape made him something of a hero in the eyes of the local youth. He was caught eight days later, exhausted and hungry, on Smugglers' Mountain, where he had been hiding. He had been living rough in abandoned shacks, living off the land, but he did not have the woodsman's skills to enable him to do this competently.

The pre-trial hearings went forward again, Bundy still conducting his own defence. It was his great good fortune that, despite the enormous pile of evidence stacked against him, most of it was purely circumstantial. It looked as though he could be the victim of some incredible chain of coincidences . . .

The court soon became impatient with the endless legal motions he used to delay the case. Bundy, too, became impatient of captivity and with a hacksaw blade carved a hole round the light fitting in the ceiling of his cell. On 30 December 1978 he hoisted himself through the foot-wide opening. He had been steadily losing weight on his special diet, and once more walked out of jail.

Rejoicing in his freedom, he took a train to Chicago, unrecognized and unchallenged. From there he went to Ann Arbor, Michigan, after which he went south to Atlanta, Georgia and Tallahassee, Florida. Here he took a room. No one had recognized him. Two blocks away were the fraternity and sorority houses for Florida State University students.

On the night of 15 January 1978 a female student caught a glimpse of a man, outside the front door, holding a log of wood. While she was wondering whether or not to call the police to report a prowler or peeping Tom, a girl named Karen Chandler staggered out of her room, bleeding heavily. She had been violently beaten about the head. So had her room-mate, Katherine Kleiner, whose jaw had been broken. In other rooms, Lisa Levy and Margaret Bowman were later found lying on their beds. Margaret was dead, having been strangled with her own tights, beaten and sexually abused. Lisa died on her way to hospital. She had also been beaten and abused.

An hour and a half later, another female student awoke in her room, a few blocks away from the Chi Omega sorority house. She had heard bangs, followed by the sounds of a girl sobbing, from the room next to hers. She dialled the girl's telephone number and the bangs stopped as the telephone began to ring. Then there was the sound of someone leaving hastily. She then called the Police, who found Cheryl Thomas, the girl in the next room, dazed and bloody, but still alive, with a fractured skull.

No one guessed that the young man named Christopher Hagen, who lived a few blocks from the scene, was in reality Ted Bundy. Had he stuck to the 'new image' of his alias, and relinquished the old 'Ted Bundy', he might well have remained in Florida for the rest of his life, with prison but a shadow in his past. His compulsive urges were his undoing.

Bundy, as 'Christopher Hagen', was not only living on borrowed time, but on stolen credit cards. On 6 February he stole a white Dodge van and left town. Two days later, in this van, he tried to pick up a schoolgirl in Jacksonville, and her brother took the licence number. That night Bundy, still using the name Christopher Hagen, stayed at a Holiday Inn, using a stolen credit card. The following day a twelve-year-old girl named Kimberly Leach walked out of her classroom to fetch something she had forgotten. She never returned.

'Christopher Hagen' returned to his lodgings in Tallahassee. He took a local girl out for an expensive meal with a stolen credit card and on the following day left his lodgings by way of the fire escape, owing large arrears of rent. He then stole an orange Volkswagen to flee the city.

Three days later, in Pensacola, a police patrolman checked the number plate of the Volkswagen and realized that it was a stolen car. Bundy tried to escape. There was a fierce but brief struggle, during which the patrolman fired a shot.

Twenty-four hours later, in police custody, 'Hagen' admitted that he was Theodore Bundy. He was arraigned on charges of stealing cars and credit cards but the police were now aware that 'Christopher Hagen' had been living in Tallahassee at the time of the sorority house attacks.

On 7 April 1978, another highway patrolman looked into an old shed near the Suwannee River State Park and saw what looked like a human foot wearing a sneaker. It was the decomposing body of Kimberly Leach. She had injuries to the pelvic region and had died from homicidal violence, including strangling and beating.

On 27 April, six lawmen subdued the struggling Bundy in order to take an impression of his teeth. It was this impression that would finally convict him. Bite marks had been found on the buttocks of Lisa Levy.

Predictably, Bundy pleaded not guilty to the sorority house outrages. In the Tallahassee courtroom Bundy continued his delaying tactics and when it became clear, as it soon did, that it would be hard to find a dozen totally unprejudiced jurors in Tallahassee, the trial was moved to Miami. Even in Miami the empanelling of the jurors took several days . . .

Although Bundy refused to confess to any of the murders, at one point during questioning he implied that the actual number of victims far exceeded the eighteen which had been attributed to him. In order to assist the court, he agreed to 'speculate freely' about the killer and his deeds. What emerged was the typical story of a loner who spent hours closeted in his room reading violent pornography bought in cheap paperback shops, which only intensified his increasing desire to commit rape accompanied by assault of the most violent nature. At the beginning of his nefarious career he became a peeping Tom, then he progressed, if that is the right word, to a 'hit-and-run' assailant. In 1973 he crept up behind a girl in the street and hit her on the head with a piece of wood. She screamed and managed to escape with only a minor wound and her attacker ran off and was never apprehended.

Only a few months later, Lynda Healy was abducted and taken to the remote area where she was raped and strangled to death.

Towards the end of his trial, however, Bundy spoke of an 'entity' – a malignant being inside himself that gradually dominated his consciousness and made rape and even murder a necessity.

The clinching testimony was provided by the dental experts, who testified that the bite marks on Lisa Levy's buttocks exactly matched the impressions of Ted Bundy's teeth – the impressions he had fought so savagely to avoid being taken that six hefty police officers had only with difficulty managed to subdue him.

On 23 July 1979 the jury, having deliberated for seven hours, found Bundy guilty of a long list of indictments. Asked whether he had anything to say, Bundy replied, 'I find it somewhat absurd to ask for mercy for something I did not do. The sentence is not a sentence of me – it is a sentence of someone who is not standing here today.'

Notwithstanding Bundy's denial, nevertheless the judge sentenced him to die in the electric chair. Seldom has 'Ol' Sparky' seated a more odious predator.

# CHAPTER THIRTEEN

## The Fat Man

As the reign of terror of one predator was drawing to a close, another equally horrific was taking his place. This monster did not prey on women and girls, but on boys and youths.

On 11 December 1978 Elizabeth Piest drove to the Nisson Pharmacy in Des Plaines, Illinois, to pick up her fifteen-year-old son Robert from his part-time after-school job, as it was her birthday and she had arranged to give him a lift home to be in time for the party she had planned. It was 9 p.m. when she arrived and Robert asked his mother to wait for a few moments while he went to see a man about another job that would pay five dollars an hour – more than twice his pay at the pharmacy. Fair enough, she thought as she settled down to wait in her car.

Mrs Piest waited half an hour and when Robert had not returned by 9.30 she drove home to inform her husband. They took turns to look for Robert and when there was still no sign of him by 11.30 they reported his disappearance to the police.

During the course of their investigations at the drugstore, the police noticed that the interior of the shop had been recently renovated. Inquiring about the contractor, they were told his name was Gacy and that he could have been the man who had offered Robert Piest a job. The police already knew of Gacy from a prior incident on their books.

A twenty-seven-year-old man named Jeffrey Rignall from Chicago had got into conversation with 'a fat man' who drove a sleek Oldsmobile. He had accepted an invitation to smoke a joint with him in his car. The man had clapped a chloroform-soaked cloth over Rignall's face, driven him to a house, and there spent several hours sodomizing him and flogging him with whips. Rignall awoke at dawn to find himself lying beside the lake in Lincoln Park. A park attendant, seeing that Rignall was in a distressed condition, took him to hospital, where it was discovered that he was bleeding from the rectum and that the chloroform which had been repeatedly administered had permanently damaged his liver.

When Rignall, sufficiently recovered, left the hospital he hired a car and spent several days looking for the 'fat man' and his black late-model Olds. Eventually his patience paid off: he saw the car, followed it, and made a note of the licence number. The car proved to belong to John Wayne Gacy. A warrant was issued for Gacy's arrest, but despite this the police still delayed acting upon it, and it was several weeks before they arrested Gacy on a misdemeanour charge. As the case dragged on, the police began to feel that if Rignall had indeed been chloroformed for much of the time he might well have been mistaken about Gacy's identity. After all, there was no shortage of fat men in Illinois – and no shortage of homosexuals either, as one police officer was quick to point out. Gacy was released for lack of conclusive evidence.

A more thorough check of Gacy's background might have caused the police to revise their views. Such a check would have revealed that he had been sentenced to ten years in prison in Waterloo, Iowa ten years previously. The charges included handcuffing an employee and attempting to sodomize him, paying a youth to perform fellatio upon him, and then hiring someone to beat up this youth when he gave evidence against Gacy in court. At that period Gacy had been married and was the manager of a fast-food take-out business. To those who had known him at that time, he was apparently a model member of the community. Described as a model prisoner, he had been paroled after a comparatively short time and placed on probation in Chicago. In 1971 he had been arrested for picking up a teenage boy and trying to force him to engage in sexual relations. The boy failed to appear in court and the case was dismissed. Another man had also accused him of trying to force him to have sexual relations with him at gunpoint. He had even boasted to this man that he had already killed somebody. Nothing came of this charge because there was no independent corroborative evidence.

The police, searching for Robert Piest, now called at Gacy's house at 8213 West Summerdale Avenue, Des Plaines, and questioned him about the missing boy. Not satisfied with Gacy's answers to their questions, they obtained a search warrant and went over his house with a fine tooth comb. Towards the end of their search, they raised a trapdoor in the floor leading to a crawlspace underneath the house. Immediately the officers were assailed by a heavy odour of decaying flesh, and the beams of their torches picked out human bones and bodies in varying stages of decomposition.

At the police station, John Wayne Gacy freely admitted that he had killed no fewer that thirty-two young boys and teenage youths after forcing them to have sexual relations with him, and stated that twenty-seven of them had been buried or otherwise disposed of in and around his house. The remaining five, including Robert Piest, had been disposed of elsewhere. Piest had been dumped in the Des Plaines River.

Seven complete bodies were found in the crawlspace under the house, and various dismembered parts of others. In another part of the house, under the floorboards, many bodies were found buried in quicklime, in trenches that had been dug in the foundations. Eight more were quickly unearthed from the back yard. Eventually Gacy's entire house had been carefully scrutinized and a total of twenty-eight bodies was accounted for. Gacy had lost count by one.

Gacy had run out of burial space in and around his house and had started dumping bodies in the river. Three bodies were recovered, including that of his last victim, Robert Piest.

This monster in human form was born on 17 March 1942 in Chicago, of Danish and Polish parentage. At the age of eleven he was struck on the head by a swing while playing in the park and suffered from recurrent blackouts from that time onwards. The cause of these was diagnosed as a blood clot on the brain which was dissolved by medical treatment. He then developed heart disease. Despite this, he attended a business college and then obtained a job as a shoe salesman. He married a co-worker whose parents owned a fried chicken business in Waterloo, Iowa. They soon installed him as manager.

Gacy was a member of the Junior Chamber of Commerce. He was known as an affable man who badly wanted to be liked and accepted, and who tried to buy popularity with generosity. On the other side of the coin, he also gained a reputation as a plausible liar and a boaster – 'the great granddaddy of all braggarts', as one of his acquaintances put it.

His married life came to an end with his imprisonment and his wife sued him for divorce. The son and daughter of the marriage remained with their mother.

In 1972 he remarried and started his own business as a contractor. His second wife found his violent tempers intolerable, his sexual performance infrequent and unsatisfactory, and then there was that persistent, peculiar odour that hung about the house . . .

In 1976 they were divorced, and Gacy continued indefatigably to try to rise in the world and impress people. He became involved with the local Democrats, he had cards printed, and in 1978 he was photographed shaking hands with President Carter's wife. Little did she realize that his contracting business was in reality little more than a respectable front to facilitate his making contact with young males.

One of these was John Butkowicz, who vanished on 1 August 1975. He may have been Gacy's first victim.

He had been doing odd jobs for Gacy and had quarrelled with him about pay. Gacy was known to be notoriously mean about wages and refused to reimburse his employees for their travelling expenses to and from their jobs. On several occasions he was known to have told them 'get yourself a bike'.

Greg Godzik came to work for Gacy sometime in 1976; on 11 December he vanished. A few weeks later, on 20 January 1977, a friend of Greg's, John Szych, vanished in mysterious circumstances. He also knew Gacy.

There were many others. In May 1976 three boys, Randall Reffett, Samuel Stapleton and Michael Bonnin, all vanished at the same time in mysterious circumstances. A month later, on 13 June, a boy named Billy Carroll disappeared and on 6 August a young high school student, Rick Johnston, was dropped off by his mother at a rock concert and was never seen again.

Once Gacy was separated from his wife, there was nothing to stop him from inviting teenage youths and schoolboys to his house. Some of these, like a young male prostitute named only as 'Jamie' in the record, were handcuffed and violently sodomized, but were allowed to go, with payment for their silence. Those who resisted were raped and killed. A nine-year-old boy was picked up off the street in the black Oldsmobile and was never seen again. The Olds became familiar in the Newtown district of Chicago, where homosexuals could be picked up in bars or on the sidewalks. Unfortunately, at that time nobody connected the 'Fat Man' with the unexplained disappearances of young boys . . . and these continued until the abduction of the thirty-third victim, Robert Piest, finally brought police with a search warrant to the house on West Summerdale Avenue.

In 1980 Gacy was sentenced to life imprisonment without possibility of parole. The 'Fat Man' will never again be able to kill young boys but this is small consolation to thirty-three grieving families.

# CHAPTER FOURTEEN

## The Citizen of the Free Universe

Dr Victor Ohta was a well-to-do physician who enjoyed a high standing in the community of Soquel, Santa Cruz County, California. He had an imposing detached house standing in well-tended grounds, the fruits of a lifetime spent in the service of the people. Dr Ohta did not have an enemy in the world. His neighbours knew that, sick or well, they could call upon him and his family at virtually any time for advice, help or medical attention in an emergency. He was available to rich and poor, black and white, the sedate businessman or the dropout hippie alike. Dr Ohta's vocabulary did not include the word discrimination.

On 19 October 1970, Dr Ohta's house was seen to be ablaze. Firemen were quickly summoned to the scene, and it was not long before they discovered five bodies in the swimming-pool in the grounds. The bodies were those of Dr Ohta, his wife Virginia, their two sons Taggart and Derrick, aged eleven and twelve respectively, and the doctor's secretary, Dorothy Cadwallader. The doctor had been shot three times and the other four had all been shot once in the back of the head, execution-style. The doctor's Rolls-Royce was parked across the drive to the house, blocking it. Under the windshield wiper was a note reading as follows:

'Hallowe'en 1970. Today, World War III will begin, as brought to you by the People of the Free Universe.

From this day forward, anyone and/or everyone or company of persons who misuses the natural environment or destroys same will suffer the penalty of death by the People of the Free Universe. I and my comrades from this day forth will fight until death or freedom against anyone who does not support natural life on this planet. Materialism must die, or mankind will stop.'

The note was signed, 'Knight of Wands, Knight of Pentacles, Knight of Cups, Knight of Swords.' The writer was evidently familiar with the Tarot pack.

Mrs Ohta's station wagon was found abandoned in a railway tunnel near the San Lorenzo River. A goods train ran into it, but as it was travelling only slowly, it merely pushed the car out of the tunnel, where it had obviously been left in the hope of causing a serious accident. The car's upholstery had been slashed and set on fire.

The murders caused panic in the area. Groups of hippies were known to be living in the nearby woods and it looked as though this might be another Manson-type killing – a protest against the 'pigs' and the bourgeoisie. Police began an intensive questioning of the various hippie commune members, but it soon became clear that the murders were not the work of a group but of one man. Quite soon, police had a suspect.

He was John Linley Frazier, a twenty-four-year-old car mechanic from Santa Cruz. For some time before the murders he had been experimenting with drugs. A bad trip on mescalin had convinced him that he had received a revelation. He left his job, separated from his wife, and went to live in an abandoned shack near one of the hippie colonies, but being strictly a loner he did not mix with them. In his lonely hut he studied the Tarot and read extensively on ecology and environmental issues. He developed a violent resentment against the materialistic society. One witness later described how Frazier had admitted to him that, some time prior to the murders, he had broken into the Ohta residence and stolen a pair of binoculars. At the time Frazier had told him that 'the Ohtas are too materialistic, and ought to be killed'. The witness had taken little notice of the remark, attributing it to the fact that Frazier was high on drugs. This witness also thought little of the burglary, since he knew that Frazier had a conviction for burglary – his only police record up to that time.

In the twenty-four hours following the crime, police appealed for anyone who had any information that could lead them to the killer to come forward. A woman reported that on the day following the murders she had seen a man of Frazier's description – small and bearded – driving Mrs Ohta's car. This led to Frazier's arrest shortly afterwards – quite soon, in fact, after he had abandoned the car in the railway tunnel and it had been pushed out by the freight train and his bid to stage a crash frustrated.

Frazier's arrest took place in a shack which he occupied near his mother's farm, which he visited from time to time. He made no admissions, and remained silent throughout his subsequent trial. His fingerprints were found on the door of the Rolls-Royce, on a beer can in the house and on other objects at the scene. This established his guilt beyond all reasonable doubt. He was sentenced to death, to join the queue of murderers awaiting execution in San Quentin's death row since the suspension of the death penalty in 1971.

All the evidence indicates that Frazier had planned the murders some days before committing them. He had given his wife his driving licence, with the comment that 'he would not be needing it again'. He told three of his hippie acquaintances that 'big things would be happening on Monday' (the day of the murders).

The police reconstructed the crime as follows. Frazier arrived at the Ohta residence some time before 3 o'clock in the afternoon on the day of the murders and held up Mrs Ohta, who was alone, with a .38 pistol. He tied her hands behind her with a scarf and took her own handgun, a .22. He then 'executed' Mrs Ohta.

Some time later, one of the teachers called Dr Ohta at

his office in town to inform him that Mrs Ohta had failed to turn up at the school to collect their younger boy, as was her usual procedure. Dr Ohta was not unduly alarmed; his wife could have had any number of reasons for not collecting him on time. But normally she would have called him at the office and also called the teachers at her son's school to notify them of any delay. Still, the doctor mused, she might be ill and unable to call. He therefore sent his secretary, Dorothy Cadwallader, to the school to collect the boy. He himself would collect the older boy later – again, this was the arrangement they had, because the older boy finished school at a later time than his brother.

Mrs Cadwallader arrived at the Ohta home with the younger son, and was met by the killer, who tied their hands behind their backs and shot them both once in the back of the head with Mrs Ohta's .22 handgun. Not long afterwards, Dr Ohta arrived with his other son. It seems that Dr Ohta put up a fight, for Frazier shot him three times with the .38 and then shot the boy once in the back of the head with the .22. He then set a fire in the house, dragged all the bodies out into the garden and dumped them into the swimming-pool. He then manoeuvred the Rolls-Royce across the drive to obstruct fire engines and police. By this time the fire had taken hold and the house was ablaze. Frazier jumped into Mrs Ohta's car and drove off.

The charge of destroying the natural environment can hardly have applied to Dr Ohta, who had taken care to leave the natural surroundings of his 300,000 dollar house untouched. Neither was Frazier's assumption that Dr Ohta was 'materialistic' true in the strictest sense of the word, for the doctor frequently gave free treatment to patients who could not afford his fees, held a free clinic for the under-privileged and was a founder-member of the Dominican Hospital in Santa Cruz. To this he contributed considerable financial support. His life had not been easy before qualifying as a doctor. He was the son of poor immigrants and had worked as a track-layer on the railways to put himself through college and then as a cab-driver to support himself while studying at medical school. The Ohtas also had two older daughters, both away at university at the time of the murders.

As in the case of Charles Manson and his 'Family', hallucinogenic drugs seem to have been to blame for a large part of John Linley Frazier's paranoid delusions. Psychiatrists, however, would also agree that an inherent mental instability probably existed in his psychic make-up in the first place. His wife said that he had once been 'a beautiful person' before he had started to dabble with drugs, after which he had turned morose, resentful and violent. Certainly the murders showed a lack of planning typical of a disoriented person with a disturbed mentality, notwithstanding that they were premeditated. Although he had a police record as a burglar, he did not take even the elementary precaution of wearing gloves and left his fingerprints both in the house and on the cars. He set the fire in the house *before* taking the five bodies out to the swimming-pool. This latter action ensured that they would be found and the bullets traced, instead of allowing the bodies to burn in the blazing house, as most other criminals would have done. Such actions were the mark of the psychopathic killer, not the carefully considered procedures of the cunning felon. Then, again, he drove off in the murdered woman's car, making no attempt whatever to conceal himself.

It did not require adroit police brains to nail John Linley Frazier as their man. Even the most bungling woodentop would have spotted him at five hundred yards.

# CHAPTER FIFTEEN

## Oedipus Revenged

Unlike John Linley Frazier, Edmund Emil Kemper began to show signs of severe psychological disturbance even as a small child. Born on 18 December 1948 and sharing with Frazier the same birthplace of Santa Cruz, California, the first known trauma of his childhood was the separation of his parents at the age of seven. He stayed with his mother, but badly missed a father's influence. Needing a man to admire and imitate as a father-figure, he became an ardent devotee of John Wayne and would frequently play truant from school in order to sit for hours in the cinema watching his hero in the movies. He joined the junior section of the Boy Scouts and, incredibly, at the tender age of eight was taught to shoot and to handle a hunting-knife while at summer camp.

By the time he was ten years old, Ed, as he was known, had developed a liking for torturing animals and was much given to fantasies about torture and death. He used to play with his young sister a make-believe game in which she had to be a 'guard' leading him to die in the gas-chamber. On one occasion he took his sister's doll and cut off its hands and feet.

As he approached puberty, it was apparent that something was also seriously wrong with the glands that regulated his physical growth and he was much bigger than the other boys of his age group. His incipient gigantism resulted in his being jeered at by his peers and he claimed that even his mother ridiculed him. He certainly grew up with a highly ambivalent attitude towards her – a kind of love-hate relationship, as he called it.

By the time he was thirteen, his sadistic fantasies were beginning to assume a more overt form. He strangled the family cat, dissected it and hid parts of its body in a wardrobe in the house, although he firmly denied that he was the perpetrator of this outrage. He even had fantasies of killing his own mother. On several occasions he went into her bedroom at night when she was asleep with a gun and toyed with the idea of shooting her, but at the last moment he always drew back and crept away. His mother had reason to be afraid of him – he grew to be 6 feet 9 inches tall and weighed twenty stone – a giant indeed, at only fifteen years of age. 'The Giant' was in fact his local nickname.

In spite of his developing sexual feelings – he had a powerful libido even when he had barely reached puberty – he was pathologically shy where women were concerned. It may have been on account of his huge size and shambling gait that he was embarrassed to ask a girl for a date as other young fellows were able to do without any difficulty. The beginnings of a deeper misogyny were surfacing. On one occasion, he told his sister that he would like to kiss a certain woman teacher at his school. 'Why don't you then?' she asked. 'You are so big she could hardly stop you!' To this, Ed replied, 'If I were to kiss her, I would have to kill her first.' In fact he now had necrophilic fantasies with increasing frequency, but his sister merely dismissed his statement about the teacher as one of his macabre jokes.

At about this time Ed ran away from home to go and live with his father, who promptly returned him to his mother. He was then sent to live with his father's parents on a ranch in California. His mother called her ex-husband to warn him that he was taking a big risk in sending Ed to live with them. 'The boy is a real weirdo,' she said, 'and will very likely end up killing someone.' His father, however, ignored this warning, to his eternal regret . . .

Ed helped his grandparents around their farm but he had a short fuse and it took very little to make him lose his temper. One day some trivial remark of his grandmother's sparked off Ed's deadly frenzy and on 24 August 1964 he picked up a .22 rifle and pointed it at his grandmother, shooting her in the back of the head. He then repeatedly stabbed her dead body with a kitchen knife.

When, a little while later, his grandfather came in from his work in the fields, Ed shot him dead before he could enter the house. He then telephoned his mother, telling her that he had just shot both his grandparents dead, and hung up. He then calmly called the police and sat in an armchair waiting for them to come and arrest him.

Ed was sent for treatment in December 1964, at the Atascadero State Hospital for the Criminally Insane, where, surprisingly, he was found to have an IQ of 136. A high intelligence quotient does not, however, automatically rule out psychotic disturbance. The noted psychiatrist Donald Lunde said of him later: 'In his way, he had avenged the rejection of both his mother and his father.'

After five years in the mental hospital he was released into the care of the California Youth Authority who, against the advice of the hospital, sent him to live with his mother in Santa Cruz, where she was working as an administrative assistant in one of the colleges of the University of California. She and Ed frequently had violent and noisy quarrels, usually over trivial matters. She told him that if he were to continue to live with her he would have to get a job. She was less concerned with the financial aspect than the fact that a job would keep him out of the house all day and give her some peace and quiet at night.

He found himself a labouring job and bought a motorcycle, which he then wrecked, suing the motorist involved, and then repeated this ploy with a second motorcycle. With the two lots of insurance money he received he bought himself a car. He now had access to the vast co-ed population of the Santa Cruz campus, many of whom used to hitch-hike to and from college and to and from the various evening activities arranged by the sororities and other college groups. He also bought several guns and knives.

153

Ed Kemper lost no time in picking up hitch-hiking co-eds for his nefarious purposes. During 1970/71 he claimed to have given lifts to more than 150 young girls, mostly college students hitch-hiking. A number of rapes, assaults and disappearances were logged by the police during this period, but remained unsolved.

On 7 May 1972 Ed committed his first known murders. He picked up Anita Luchese and Mary Ann Pesce, both students at Fresno State College in Berkeley. He produced a gun, drove to a secluded spot, and made Anita climb into the trunk of the car while he handcuffed Mary Ann and put a plastic bag over her head. Mary Ann seemed unafraid of him and tried to talk him out of what he was doing, pointing out that he could be in very serious trouble if he harmed her or her friend, but to no avail. He stabbed her in the back a number of times, then several times in the abdomen, and finally cut her throat. He then opened the trunk of the car and stabbed the other girl to death.

In the secluded wooded canyon, he gave full rein to his necrophilic compulsions, the fearful urges that impelled him to kill, maim and mutilate before he could satisfy his lust. With a living woman, he would have been impotent; only when confronted with an unresisting corpse could he respond. Psychologically, the feeling of power and dominance over a passively unresisting woman was transformed into a frenzied sexual assault on a dead one.

With the two bodies in the trunk of the car, he drove home, and finding his mother out, he stuffed the bodies into rubbish-bags and hoisted them over his shoulder, one at a time, as though he were merely removing sacks of rubbish from his car. His powerful 280-pound frame made light work of them both, and he carried them up to his room, where he spent the rest of the afternoon in the grisly work of decapitating and dismembering the bodies. He carried out necrophilic acts on the headless bodies before dissecting them. He then consigned the dismembered bodies to plastic sacks and under cover of darkness carried them out to his car while his mother was watching TV. He drove out to the mountains and buried the sacks under rocks, then washed his car with water from a stream to remove any bloodstains, and went home. His mother was used to his coming and going at all hours of the day or night and thought nothing of his late return. At least when he was out he was not annoying her with his violent tempers and shouting . . . but she had no inkling of his horrendous activities.

On 14 September 1972 he picked up fifteen-year-old Aiko Koo, a Japanese high school student, as she was hitch-hiking to a dance class in San Francisco. He produced a gun, drove her into the mountains, stopped the car and then taped her mouth. When he attempted to suffocate her by putting his fingers up her nostrils, she put up a fierce fight, but, her air supply cut off, she died quickly. He took her from the car and laid her on the ground, where he raped her, achieving orgasm within seconds. He took her back to his room, cut off her head and, becoming highly aroused, had sexual intercourse with the decapitated body. Afterwards he cut off the hands and dismembered the torso, and took the remains out to the mountains above Boulder Creek, where he buried them.

On 8 January 1973 an unsuspecting girl student named Cynthia Schall, unperturbed to see a giant nearly seven feet tall at the wheel of the car she had thumbed, climbed into the passenger seat and was driven, as she thought, along the road to her destination, Cabrillo College. Producing a gun, he drove to the little town of Freedom, where he stopped on a quiet side road. For a while he played a cat-and-mouse game with her, telling her that he had no intention of harming her. As he held the gun on her, he was obviously enjoying the sensation of knowing she was helpless and in his power. Then he shot her, put her body into the trunk of his car, and drove home.

Cynthia Schall was a big, heavy girl, and even Ed Kemper staggered as he hoisted her up to his room. He placed her in his closet and when his mother came home he talked to her, and behaved perfectly normally. As soon as his mother had left for work the following morning, Ed removed the body from the closet and engaged in various sexual acts. He dissected it in the shower with an axe, and then drove out to Carmel with various parts of the body in plastic rubbish-bags and threw them off various cliffs. This time parts of the body were discovered only a day later, and identified as Cynthia Schall's remains. Panic now ensued as murder was added to the list of disappearances, rapes and assaults of co-eds in the area, with police still unable to name a suspect.

After a particularly violent quarrel with his mother on 5 February 1973, Ed Kemper drove to the local campus and picked up Rosalind Thorpe, who was just coming out of a lecture which had formed part of a series of evening seminars. Shortly afterwards he picked up another student, twenty-one-year-old Alice Lui, who had been attending another evening class elsewhere in the college building. As they drove along in the dark, ostensibly towards a nearby small town where both girls lived, Ed suddenly produced a gun and shot Rosalind through the head. As Alice Lui covered her face with her hands, he shot her several times in the head. Then he stopped the car and put both bodies in the trunk. On arriving home he found his mother was in, and he could not risk carrying them into the house, so he left them outside still in the trunk of his car. But his sexual excitement was too intensely aroused to allow him to wait for a more propitious moment. He took his big hunting knife, which he called 'the General', and under cover of darkness he hacked off both heads from the bodies while they were still in the trunk of the car.

The following morning, after his mother had left for work, he carried the headless body of Alice Lui into the shower, washed off the blood, and engaged in necrophilic relations with the decapitated corpse. He then carried the other body into the house and washed it, although in his subsequent confession it was never made clear whether he violated it in similar fashion. He then returned the bodies to his car, cut off Alice Lui's hands, and then drove on to the Coast Highway south of Pacifia, where he disposed of the heads and afterwards dumped the bodies in Eden Canyon, Alameda, where they were found by hunters nine days later.

Some time after this, a police officer routinely checking through the gun licences realized that one registered gun owner, Edmund Emil Kemper, had a criminal record, but had not declared this when filling out the mandatory application form. He drove to Kemper's home and found him outside in his car with a young blonde girl. Kemper handed over the gun, and the police officer drove off. This probably saved the life of the blonde, who left the car precipitately during the interview.

Kemper had an increasing pressure inside his head, a feeling that he was soon going to 'blow up' and commit a crime which would result in his being unavoidably caught. He decided to kill his own mother. On the morning of Easter Sunday, 1973, he entered his mother's bedroom and hit her on the head, with a hammer. He then cut off her head with 'the General' and hid the body in his closet. He then felt sick, and needed fresh air, so he went for a drive in his car. Seeing an acquaintance who owed him 10 dollars, he left his own car and went for a drive in his friend's car. This man gave him the 10 dollars. 'This probably saved his life,' Kemper said in his confession later. 'I had felt the need to kill someone else at that point, but as he had returned my loan I could hardly kill him then.'

On returning home, he still felt a surging need to kill another person, so he called a friend of his mother's, Sarah Hallett, and invited her round to dinner that evening with himself and his mother. When she arrived at the appointed hour, Ed strangled her, after first knocking her unconscious with a brick. This was followed by the usual ritual decapitation and violation of the body.

That night he slept in his mother's bed. His mother's body was still in the closet in the adjoining room . . .

The next day he drove west in Mrs Hallett's car. Then,

using money he had taken from the dead woman's handbag, he rented a Hertz car. At one point he was stopped by a highway patrolman for speeding and fined 25 dollars on the spot. The police officer did not see the gun which Ed had on the rear seat. Ed had been expecting to be the subject of a manhunt but when after another three days there was still no news on radio or TV or in the newspapers of the finding of the bodies of his two latest victims, he stopped in Pueblo, Colorado, and called the police, saying that he was the 'Co-ed Killer' they had been looking for. The officer who took the call dismissed him as a crank and merely told him to call back later. He did, several times, but it was only after a number of calls that he finally convinced them that he was not a crackpot but in deadly earnest . . . And still, only half-believing the wild story, they sent just one rookie patrolman to arrest him.

In custody in Pueblo, Edmund Emil Kemper proved to be more than eager to talk. He described his killings in minute detail, even as to the extent of explaining how he had buried the head of one of his victims in the garden, facing towards the house so that he could imagine her looking at him, and how he had cut out his mother's voice-box and dropped it into the dustbin 'because it seemed appropriate after she had bitched and nagged me non-stop all the time'. He explained that he had driven to Pueblo before turning himself in because, he said, if he had gone to the local police 'they might shoot first and ask questions later'. Incongruously, he added that he was 'terrified of violence'.

He related a horrifying catalogue of sadism, mutilation, murder, necrophilia and even cannibalism, though this latter was never proved. He admitted killing six co-eds, graphically describing their murder, decapitation and burial, as well as the murders of his mother and her friend. Even hardened detectives were visibly shocked at the confession which poured from the giant's lips.

Kemper was arraigned at Santa Cruz in April 1973 on

eight counts of murder, and adjudged to be legally sane, though many would disagree. He was sentenced to life imprisonment without the possibility of parole, although he had asked for the death penalty. Perhaps he had felt that, now that he had resolved his basic inner conflict in his own way, he no longer had the need to go on living.

# CHAPTER SIXTEEN

## Travels with a Shotgun

Paul John Knowles was a petty crook, car thief and burglar who spent an average of six months out of every year in prison from 1965, when he was nineteen, to 1972. He was serving a longer term in Raiford Penitentiary, Florida, when he began to study astrology and started corresponding with Angela Kovac, a divorcee whom he had contacted through the magazine *American Astrology*. After a while, she flew to Florida to visit him in prison and hired a lawyer to work on his parole. She also agreed to marry him. The efforts of the lawyer to arrange his parole took some time, but eventually Knowles was freed on 14 May 1974.

The tall, red-haired twenty-five-year-old flew to San Francisco to meet his future wife, full of hopes and ambitions. It seemed, however, that these latter did not include turning over a new leaf. Burglary still seemed to him an easier way of making a living than taking an honest job. Angela Kovac had, prior to his release, fixed up a job for him with a firm run by one of her relatives. Knowles meanwhile was trying to work out in his mind how best to get out of this situation. After all, he could not afford to be undiplomatic; Angela had a beautiful apartment in the Bay City, a prestigious job with a steady income, had promised to marry him and, what was most important, had gone to a great deal of trouble and expense to get him out of prison.

In the meantime, a friend who was a psychic medium told Angela that 'she had a very dangerous man in her life', and when Knowles turned up at her apartment, she began to experience a deep, instinctive unease – call it woman's intuition if you like. This made her change her mind about marrying him. She sent him to stay at her mother's while she came to a final decision. Her mother said that she liked him and thought he would make a good husband once he had pulled himself together and shown that he could keep a steady job. But after four days Angela decided against the marriage and told him that she could not go through with it. He took this news rather badly but did not make a scene. Collecting up his belongings from his erstwhile fiancée's mother's apartment, he returned to Florida.

Much later, Knowles told his lawyer that on the night Angela had jilted him he had gone out on to the streets of San Francisco and killed three people. This, however, was never verified. After Knowles had left, Angela became reconciled with her ex-husband and when Knowles called her from Florida she told him she did not wish to see him again.

In Florida, he got into a fight in a bar and was locked up in Jacksonville Police Station. He picked the lock and escaped. Later that same evening, on 26 July 1974, Knowles broke into the home of a sixty-five-year-old teacher, Alice Curtis, intent on burglary. He bound and gagged her, stole her money and her car. What he did not realize at that time was that he had rammed the gag too deep into her mouth, suffocating her to death. He was later to say that he had never intended this: 'I just tied up the old woman and gagged her to keep her quiet when I burgled the joint.'

Despite the widespread dragnet out for him, Jacksonville seemed to exert a fascination for him and he stayed on there for several days. This was even after police had linked him to the Curtis murder and his description had been announced on radio and TV as well as in all the newspapers. He was still driving the stolen car. One night he was parked in a quiet street when he observed two young girls staring at him. Their mother was a friend of his family and the two girls had recognized him. Knowles

161

forced them into the car and drove off. The bodies of Mylette Anderson, seven, and her eleven-year-old sister Lillian were later found in a swamp a few miles out of Jacksonville.

The following day Knowles drove to Atlantic Beach, Florida, broke into the home of Marjorie Howe and strangled her with one of her own nylon stockings. He stole her TV set. A few days later he picked up a teenage girl hitch-hiker who told him that she was a runaway. Knowles later claimed that he had taken her into the woods, raped her and then strangled her. Several weeks later the decomposed body of a young girl was found in the general area, but it was never positively identified.

On 23 August he broke into the home of Cathie Pierce of Musella, Florida and strangled her with a telephone cord while her three-year-old looked on helplessly. He left the boy unharmed. For the next three days he stayed around the Musella area. When someone reported seeing the stolen car he was still driving, he left.

On 3 September, near Lima, Ohio, Knowles struck up a conversation with an accounts executive, one William Bates, and they had several drinks together at Scott's Inn. They left together at midnight and Bates was not seen again until a month later when his strangled naked body was found in some woods not far away. Nearby was the abandoned stolen car. Knowles had driven off in the dead man's white Impala.

Using Bates's money and credit cards, Knowles went to Sacramento, California, and then to Seattle, then back East into Utah. In Ely, Nevada, he saw a camping trailer in a quiet location on 18 September, and forced an entry. The elderly couple, who were on vacation from San Pedro, were later found shot through the head. They were Emmett and Lois Johnson. Knowles took their money and credit cards and headed out of the area.

Three days after this, he saw a woman in a car beside the road near Sequin, Nevada. He pulled in, ordered her out of the car, and raped and strangled her. He then dragged the body through a barbed wire fence.

On 23 September – only two days after killing his last victim – he was in Birmingham, Alabama, where he met an attractive woman named Ann Dawson, who owned a beauty shop in Fairfield. The two seemed to have taken a liking to one another, for during the next six days they travelled around together – on her money. He killed her on 29 September, but her body has never been found.

For more than a fortnight Knowles spent his time driving around through Oklahoma, Missouri, Iowa and Minnesota, without apparently committing any more crimes, apart from the fact that he was still driving a stolen car and using stolen cash and credit cards. By 16 October he had arrived in Marlboro, Connecticut and on an impulse parked outside a house he liked the look of and rang the doorbell. The door was opened by a pretty schoolgirl, fifteen-year-old Dawn Wein, who broke off her school homework to open the door, thinking it was a girl friend from her high school class. Knowles forced his way into the house at gunpoint and frogmarched the girl up to her bedroom where he spent the next hour raping her. Her mother, Mrs Karen Wein, then returned from a shopping trip and Knowles forced her to cook him a meal at gunpoint, after which he ordered mother and daughter into the bedroom, forced them both to strip and tied their hands behind their backs. After raping Mrs Wein several times, he then strangled each of them with a nylon stocking. He left with Dawn's collection of rock records and a tape-recorder. The bodies were found later that evening by Mrs Wein's other daughter.

Knowles now headed south and 19 October found him in Virginia. In Woodford, a small town south of Fredericksburg, he chose a house at random and knocked at the door, just as he had done in Marlboro, Connecticut. The door was opened by fifty-three-year-old Doris Hovey. He told her that he would not harm her, but he needed a gun. Mrs Hovey unlocked her husband's gun cabinet and gave him a .22 rifle. Knowles loaded it and shot her through the head. He then wiped the weapon clean of

163

fingerprints, left it on the floor beside the body and left the house without taking anything. That had been purely a killing for pleasure . . .

Knowles now drove to Key West, Florida. He was still driving the white Impala he had stolen from William Bates. He picked up two girl hitch-hikers, intending to kill them, but was stopped by a highway patrolman for pulling up on a bend, which is illegal on US highways. Knowles fully expected to be arrested, but the patrolman merely glanced at his driving documents and motioned him to carry on, with just a warning. That patrolman's inefficiency was to cost more lives . . .

Knowles dropped the two hitch-hikers off in Miami and called his lawyer, Sheldon Yawitz. The experience with the patrolman had shaken him severely. It had been a very close shave. He toyed with the idea of giving himself up. 'What would you say,' he told Yawitz, 'if I were to confess to fourteen murders?' 'I wouldn't believe you,' the lawyer replied. Knowles decided to tape his own confession, using the tape-recorder he had stolen from the Wein house.

On 6 November, in a gay bar in Macon, Georgia, Knowles met a man named Caswell Carr. They had a few drinks and Carr invited his new acquaintance to spend the night at his home. Later that evening an argument developed between them and Carr's daughter was awakened by the shouting. She went downstairs to find Knowles standing over the body of her father, whom he had stabbed to death. Knowles strangled the fifteen-year-old girl, tried unsuccessfully to rape her after death and left the house, again without stealing anything.

There were almost certainly more victims between the time that Knowles left Miami and the night of the Carr murders. In woods near Macon, police found the body of a hitch-hiker, Edward Hilliard, and also items belonging to Deborah Griffin who had been hitch-hiking with him. Her body was never found. Forensic pathologists determined that Hilliard had been killed about four days before the Carr killings.

164

In Atlanta, Georgia, on 8 November, Knowles met an English journalist named Sandy Fawkes. He spent a considerable amount of time with her. They drove around and stayed together in various motels. At no time did he try to harm her, but, with hindsight, she knows she is lucky to be still alive. She recognized him for what he was – a disturbed, lonely and frightened individual hiding behind a mask of bravado. She has written a most detailed and moving book, *Killing Time*, about her experiences with this man who could have shot her dead at any time.*

Later that month, in Atlanta, Knowles offered a lift to a woman who was late for an appointment with her hairdresser. On the way, she noticed that he had taken a wrong turning. He told her that he wanted to have sexual intercourse with her and would not harm her if she complied. When she demurred, he stopped the car and pointed a gun at her. She managed to escape from the car and ran along the road, waving her arms to attract the attention of an oncoming motorist, who picked her up as Knowles drove off at speed. The girl managed to remember part of the licence plate number of the Impala and called the police. Later, a patrol car spotted the white Impala and tried to overtake it and force the driver to pull in. As he drew alongside, Knowles wound down the offside window and pointed a sawn-off shotgun at the patrolman. The latter considered discretion to be the better part of valour and quickly dropped behind, and managed to lose his quarry. This action undoubtedly saved his life.

Knowles's next stop was in West Palm Beach, Florida. He knew that he must at all costs get rid of the Impala. He stopped at random and knocked on a door in Locust Street, which was opened by a woman in a wheelchair named Beverly Mabee. He told her that he was from the Internal Revenue Service so that she would allow him to enter. Once inside, he dropped the pretence and told her that he needed a car. She told him that her twin sister Barbara was out with

* FAWKES, Sandy. *Killing Time*. (Taplinger, New York 1979)

the family Volkswagen. Knowles told Beverly that he would wait until Barbara returned. When she came home, accompanied by her six-year-old son, Knowles tied up the boy and Beverly Mabee but took Barbara as a hostage.

That night, Knowles took his captive in her car to a motel in Fort Pierce, Florida. He kept her there with him all the next day and part of the night, when, leaving her tied up, he drove off in her car. Barbara managed to escape and gave police a description of her car and of the man who had kidnapped her.

The next morning a patrolman named Campbell spotted a car which matched the given description but had some difficulty in identifying it as the missing car because Knowles had changed the licence plates. On trying to overtake the suspect car, he, like the previous patrolman, found himself looking at the wrong end of a sawn-off shotgun. Knowles forced him to a stop at gunpoint, handcuffed him with his own handcuffs, and then made him sit in the rear seat of his patrol car. He then drove off, but the brakes were poor, the suspension left much to be desired, and the car's general performance was not to his liking. Using the police siren, he forced another car, driven by businessman James Meyer, to pull over. Knowles handcuffed him, forced him to sit in the rear of the car, and then ordered the captive patrolman to join him at gunpoint. Knowles then drove off at speed.

In Pulaski County, he stopped the car in a wood, forced his victims at gunpoint to get out of the car, and handcuffed them to a tree. He then shot them both in the back of the head.

Still in Georgia, Knowles spotted a police roadblock ahead. He accelerated through it, but skidded and lost control of the car, which crashed into a tree. Knowles leapt out unhurt and ran into the woods. Two hundred policemen with tracker dogs and helicopters searched for him, but he was eventually spotted from the window of a house by a young man named Terry Clark. He grabbed his shotgun and went out to try to apprehend the fugitive, not knowing

166

whether he was armed or not. Knowles, who had left his own weapon in the car, gave himself up without a struggle. It was 17 November 1974. His murderous spree had lasted almost four months and had cost at least eighteen lives.

Knowles made a preliminary appearance in court and gave various newspaper interviews. One journalist noted that Knowles always looked very pleased with himself and was observed smiling almost continuously. He was having his hour of glory, the journalist wrote later. The daily stories of the women in his life had made newsmen dub him the 'Casanova Killer', and every new story of a woman's submission to his will made 'hot copy'. He had become a folk villain overnight. The long years of loneliness, failure and rejection had been blotted out; he had an identity now. He was already being referred to as 'the most heinous killer in American history'. In one newspaper, he was quoted as saying that he was 'the only successful member of his family', and to another columnist he was alleged to have said that he had actually committed thirty-five murders, but since this could not be proved and was probably an exaggeration, this story was not published.

The day after his capture, when Knowles was in the process of being transferred to a maximum security jail, he picked the lock of the handcuff with which he was shackled to his police guard and made a grab for the sheriff's gun. FBI agent Ron Angel shot him dead. By violence he had lived, and by violence he was to die.

# CHAPTER SEVENTEEN

## 'For Heaven's Sake Catch Me'

From a killer of eighteen people to a killer of three people seems like an improvement. But this killer of three was barely seventeen years of age when he killed, horribly mutilated and dismembered his last victim – who was little more than one-third of his age.

William Heirens was born in 1929 in Lincolnwood, a suburb of Chicago, Illinois, the product of an upper middle-class background. Slightly-built, he was five feet ten inches tall, dark-haired and brown-eyed, which made him a target for girls with an eye to good-looking guys, but they left him cold. He had what can only be described as a horror of normal sexual relationships, which probably derived, at least in part, from the repressive atmosphere of his puritanical home. He avoided dating and other social contacts with girls, which led to speculation that he was gay, but such was far from the case, as his subsequent history shows.

As early as at nine years of age he began stealing women's underwear from neighbourhood clothes-lines, but, as he told a psychiatrist later, 'I did not understand why I used to do it.' He was a solitary child, sensitive, and difficult to get to know. Apparently no one ever got close enough to him to establish a real relationship with him. He was afraid of his parents, especially his father, who seemed to be distant and far removed from daily life, while his mother was forbidding and strait-laced. In the seventh and eighth grades, his teachers noted that he was given to 'excessive daydreaming', yet this did not, it seems, prevent him from becoming a brilliant student later in his academic career.

When he was eleven years old, he inadvertently came across a couple engaged in sexual congress and found this a very traumatic experience. Unable to understand what it was all about, he confided it to his mother and asked her to explain. Her reply was, 'All sex is dirty. If you touch anyone like that, you get a disease.' This experience and his mother's reaction was a profoundly inhibiting influence on him, and resulted in a sheer physical repugnance to sexual relations with women. When he was seventeen and already at university, he was profoundly shocked when he observed other young men smuggling girls into their rooms, or necking with them in parked cars. He made an effort to overcome his revulsion by petting with a girl but he shamed himself in her eyes by bursting into tears and vomiting. He at once decided that this was an activity he did not wish to pursue any further.

He had, however, long before this, discovered one thing that did give him sexual fulfilment, and that was burglary. He had gone from stealing underwear from clothes-lines to breaking into houses looking for such items in bedrooms, bathrooms and laundry-baskets, and had burgled a good many houses by the time he was twelve and approaching puberty, which came early to him. During these burglaries, he discovered that the act of breaking into a house by entering through an open window was enough to cause him to have a violent erection, and as he climbed through he would frequently ejaculate. Psychiatrists were later to theorize that the open window he entered symbolized a woman, but he himself at the time was at a loss to explain the reason for his bizarre perversion.

When Heirens was thirteen, on the eve of his graduation from the eighth grade at St Mary's of the Lake parochial school in Chicago, he had his first brush with the law. The police picked him up for carrying a loaded pistol. He confessed to detectives that he had committed eleven burglaries and set six fires in the months immediately preceding his apprehension. Since he rarely stole from the houses he broke into, the police were at a loss to know the motive, and put it down to boyish devilment. Police searched his home and found a veritable arsenal of weapons secreted about the premises, including on the roof. There was an army rifle, a 25mm calibre pistol, and two .38 revolvers; the weapons found on the roof were four more pistols and another rifle. And this boy was only thirteen! His parents were amazed: they had no inkling whatsoever of the cache.

Police also found pictures of Adolf Hitler, Goering, Himmler and other Nazis in his room, and various books on perversions such as sadism and masochism, flagellation and bondage. Again, his parents had no knowledge of these items.

When Heirens appeared in the juvenile court he showed some apparent remorse, whether real or feigned is hard to say. After his parents had agreed to send him to a private correctional institute in Indiana, he was placed on probation. After a year in this school, he was permitted to transfer to St Bede's Academy in Peru, Illinois, where he remained for three years. He was far above average as a student, and from there entered the University of Chicago, skipping the entire freshman year to enrol as a sophomore. Throughout this time, Heirens continued his burglary forays, but so rarely was anything taken that many of the owners or tenants of the houses and apartments he broke into declined to report the incidents. As Heirens was later to tell psychiatrists, 'I get sexual satisfaction just from breaking into a place. I would get a real thrill. That would be much more satisfying to me than taking anything. People would leave money around, jewellery, valuable watches. But I very rarely ever took anything.' It may have made sense, of a kind, to the psychiatrists, but the police were completely flummoxed. What kind of a weirdo was this guy?

Heirens went over the edge from burglary and into his first murder in June 1945. Previous to this, he had on one occasion slashed a woman's throat and stabbed her several times after disturbing her from sleep during a burglary, but she recovered. He vanished down a fire escape and was never apprehended for this attack. On another occasion the owner of the apartment was disturbed by a noise Heirens made when he inadvertently tripped over a footstool, but Heirens managed to knock him out with a chair and make good his escape. However, when he entered the apartment of forty-three-year-old Mrs Josephine Alice Ross in June, he began to ransack the flat looking for feminine under-garments, and the sleeping divorcee was awakened by the noise. He slashed her throat, nearly decapitating her, and stabbed the dead body fourteen times.

The large amount of blood seemed to disturb Heirens a great deal. He went into the bathroom and came back with wet towels which he tied around the dead woman's neck, in an effort to staunch the flow. The wound still bled and was still visible, and, feeling more and more disturbed, he looked for a red garment with which to cover his victim's bloody body and make the gore less conspicuous. In a closet he found a red dress, which he wrapped tightly around the body. He then took 12 dollars from her purse and stayed two hours in the apartment, pacing from room to room. In his later confession, he stated that his role as an intruder caused him to ejaculate several times. Heirens then left the apartment, passing the murdered woman's daughter, Jacqueline Miller, on the stairs as she was returning from work.

In October of the same year Heirens broke into the flat of a US Army nurse, Lieutenant Evelyn Peterson. She discovered him in the bedroom rifling through a chest of drawers. Grabbing a chair, he hit her on the head and made his escape.

One evening soon after this attack, a thirty-three-year-old US Women's Navy officer named Frances Brown came out of her bathroom to find Heirens in her bedroom rifling her purse. He had entered her flat via an unlocked window after climbing the fire escape. As she began screaming, Heirens fired two shots from a .38 automatic at point-blank range, killing her instantly. Heirens then went into the kitchen and took a butcher's knife and returned to the bedroom to stab the girl's body in two places, leaving the knife embedded in the second wound.

Frances Brown's blood-soaked body was once again a source of great mental disturbance to her killer. He dragged the corpse into the bathroom and washed off the blood, and covered the body with wet towels, as he had done on the previous occasion. He then covered the body with a dressing-gown which had been hanging on the bathroom door, and left the dead girl lying on the floor half in and half out of the bathroom.

Police later summoned to the flat found that although the killer had taken great pains to wipe away all fingerprints from the bedroom he had omitted to take the precaution of doing the same thing in the bathroom, and they found a clear complete set on the bathroom door, 'as good as any set of police dabs', as one officer later said. In the bedroom, they also discovered a terrifying message, written in lipstick, on the mirror:

FOR HEAVEN'S SAKE CATCH ME BEFORE I KILL MORE. I CANNOT CONTROL MYSELF.

This had the inevitable result of the unknown assailant becoming known as 'the Lipstick Killer' in the Press. And the Chief of Detectives warned his men, 'This man has killed twice, and he will keep on killing until we catch him. We are working against time.'

On 7 January 1946 Heirens entered an apartment on Chicago's North Side, and as he dropped from the window-ledge to the floor of the bedroom he had entered, six-year-old Suzanne Degnan awoke. The tenant of the flat immediately above, Ethel Hargrove, was later to tell police that she was awakened by a disturbance coming from the flat below, and looking at her bedside alarm clock noticed that the time was 12.50 a.m. Quite clearly, this witness said, she heard the child, whom she knew, say, 'I don't want to get up – I want to sleep.'

Heirens gagged the child and hoisted her over his shoulder. To enter the flat he had made a makeshift ladder, which he had left outside the window partly concealed by some shrubbery. He clambered out of the window and down this ladder with Suzanne kicking and struggling but unable to cry out.

When police were called, on the child's parents finding her missing from her bed early the next morning, officers found a note reading as follows:

GET $20,000 READY AND WAIT FOR WORD.
DO NOT NOTIFY FBI OR POLICE. BILLS IN
5s AND 10s.

On the reverse side was a postscript which read:

BURN THIS FOR HER SAFETY.

Once out of the house, Heirens carried the child, still protesting, into the basement of a nearby house, and there killed her, by what method is not known. He then hideously mutilated and dismembered the body, wrapping the parts in the dead child's pyjamas and parts of a bedsheet he had wrapped round her when carrying her out of the house. He then walked around the streets in the pre-dawn half-light, dropping the grisly remains through the various gratings that led to the city's underground sewers. A soldier later testified he saw Heirens walking about a block away from the Degnan residence at about 1 a.m. carrying a holdall (which probably contained the rolled-up rope-ladder and burglary tools), and a janitor in the vicinity, about his early-morning chores, also noticed 'a youth wandering aimlessly about, and carrying something'.

Heirens had left his fingerprints all over Suzanne's bedroom, which was unusual for him – not his *modus operandi* at all. Neither was any further ransom demand made; police in fact discounted the theory that the ransom had been a serious intention – more of a red herring, and a clumsy one at that. They came to the conclusion that the kidnapper probably did not know either the family's name or their address, and that the 'ransom note' was more probably the product of a disordered mind.

In one of the most intensive manhunts Chicago had ever known, police soon found parts of Suzanne Degnan's body and also the murder knife, but they still had to find the perpetrator of this outrage. It was not until more than five months later, on 26 June 1946, that their search came to an end.

That night, a North Side apartment house janitor reported a prowler in the vicinity of his building. Detective T.P. Constant took the call. The detective found the janitor and one of the tenants, a Mrs Leona Pera, grappling with a youth, who managed to break away from them and held them at bay with a loaded pistol. Constant moved in, and the youth fired two shots at him, narrowly missing him on each occasion. The detective lunged towards Heirens, and the two struggled until, by chance, an off-duty policeman named Abner Cunningham, who had been for an early-evening swim in the nearby lake and was wearing only his bathing trunks, saw them as he was returning to his flat in the block. Grabbing a heavy earthenware plant tub from the ornamental garden in front of the building, he crashed it down on Heirens's head, which subdued him sufficiently to allow him to be handcuffed by the detective and taken into custody.

At the police station, Heirens was injected with sodium pentothal (the so-called truth drug) and interrogated. Unknown to them, however, Heirens had for the past nine months been injecting himself regularly with this drug, so that he had almost total immunity to it. In answer to the detectives' various questions, Heirens implicated another person whose name, he said, was George Murman. It soon became clear that 'George Murman' was Heirens's *alter ego*, existing only in his own mind, and that 'Murman' was, psychiatrists later theorized, really a contraction of 'murder man'. The killer's second name was George. The replies to the interrogators' questions described the burglaries and the killings as well as their locations, and Heirens would frequently remark, 'George has been a very bad boy'. It was a classic example of a schizophrenic or 'Jekyll and Hyde' personality – the real killer displacing all his crimes and their associated burden of guilt on to his 'other self'.

The fingerprints in the death apartments, the handwriting of the anguished cry for help written in lipstick, and the handwriting of the ransom note, all matched those of the suspect. At his arraignment and trial a plea of insanity was put forward, and from evidence given it was abundantly clear that latent insanity had indeed been present in the accused man since early childhood, this was put forward in mitigation, as well as his youth – he was barely seventeen years old.

Heirens was given three consecutive life sentences for his three murders, which he is presently serving in Joliet Penitentiary. Three consecutive life sentences ensure that he will never be released, as he will never be eligible for parole. As he wrote in his victim's lipstick in desperation that he could not control himself, he is now in an environment where others can control him. At least the streets of Chicago are a safer place, but have the doctors and the drugs been able to eliminate 'George Murman' from William Heirens's tortured mind?

# CHAPTER EIGHTEEN

## The Zodiac Killer

It seems that Paul John Knowles, whose murderous career we traced in Chapter Sixteen, was not the only killer to have been interested in astrology, for the 'Zodiac Killer', as he was known, certainly studied the stars. He was more or less contemporaneous with Knowles, although he covered less ground. Between 20 December 1968 and 11 October 1969 the Zodiac Killer committed five known murders – there were probably several more – and seriously wounded two other persons. Unfortunately, it was the police who had no luck at all, either in their stars or otherwise, and the Zodiac murders remain unsolved to this day.

On 20 December 1968 a woman driving from Vallejo to Benica, near San Francisco, noticed a parked station wagon with two bodies lying in the road nearby. She drove into town and called police, who found a teenage boy lying dead beside the vehicle. He had been shot through the head. Some distance away lay the body of a girl who had been shot several times in the back. It would seem that these shots had been fired as she had tried to escape from the killer by running along the road. The dead boy was identified as David Faraday, a high school student, and the girl was Betty Lou Jensen. The spot where they were found was known as a 'lovers' lane'. The killings appeared to be completely motiveless since the boy's wallet containing cash was still intact in his jacket pocket, and the girl had not been sexually interfered with in any way. The police were completely mystified. No witnesses could be traced and the killings were assigned to the unsolved case file.

On 5 July 1969 a man with a gruff voice called the Vallejo Police Department. 'I wish to report a double murder,' he said. 'If you will go one mile east on Columbus Parkway to a public park, you will find the kids in a brown car. They have been shot with a 9mm Luger. I also killed those kids last year. Good-bye!'

The police found the car exactly as the caller had directed them. In the car they found a seriously-wounded young man, Michael Mageau, and a dead girl, Darlene Ferrin, the mother of a young child.

Mageau was later able to tell police that he and Darlene Ferrin had driven into the parking lot when a car drove up and came to a halt beside them. It drove off, but returned ten minutes later, and someone – presumably the driver – shone a powerful torch into their faces, blinding them both. This person then walked up to their car and without a word started shooting. Mageau described the assailant's figure as stockily-built, about five feet eight inches, white, round-faced with wavy light brown hair, and aged about twenty-five to thirty. Witnesses were found who had seen the killer's car driving off at speed after the shooting.

On 1 August the Vallejo *Times-Herald* and two San Francisco newspapers each received a letter, signed with a cross surmounting a circle – the sign of the Zodiac. The letters described the killings in a wealth of detail that would have been impossible for anyone who had not actually committed them. The letters also contained some kind of code or cipher. The writer stated that if the ciphers to all three of the letters were put together, his identity would be made known. He also threatened to go on the rampage if his letters were not published, and kill a dozen people.

A code expert deciphered the cryptic lines, which read:

I like to kill people because it is so much fun. It is more fun than killing wild game in the forest, because Man is the most dangerous animal of all. To kill something gives me the most thrilling experience. It is even better than [sex] . . . The best part [will be] when I die. I will be reborn in Paradise, and then all I have killed will become my slaves. I will not give you my name, because you will try to slow or stop my collecting of slaves for my after-life.

The publication of these letters produced more than a thousand leads from people who thought they might know the Zodiac Killer's identity, but none of them led anywhere.

On 27 September a man with a gruff voice rang the Napa Police Department and said that he wanted to report a double murder. Police hastened to the shores of Lake Verriesa, where they had been directed and found a man and woman in a car, both suffering from stab wounds and bleeding copiously. In the car police found scrawls which included the sign of the Zodiac. The two victims, Cecilia Shepard and Bryan Hartnell, were both students at Pacific Union College. Hartnell was still alive, and was able to tell police how they had been accosted by a man wearing a hood with eye-slits cut in it and the sign of the Zodiac on it in white. He carried a pistol and a knife, and demanded money. Through the eye-slits in the hood Hartnell could see the dark frames of spectacles and he also noticed that the man had light brown hair. He also said that the man was 'pudgy' in build.

The man had then bound the two students and then told them, 'I am going to stab you people.' He was as good as his word . . .

From the telephone, near the Napa Police Headquarters, from which the attacker had made his call, the police were able to lift three fingerprints, but these did not match any already existing in police records, and failed to lead to the killer. All they knew was that he did not have a police record.

Two weeks later, on 11 October, the killer shot a cab-driver named Paul Stein in the back of the head at Nob Hill in San Francisco, then calmly walked off, taking his victim's wallet and also a fragment torn from his shirt. The bullet was found to have come from the same gun that had killed Darlene Ferrin.

The next day the *San Francisco Chronicle* received another Zodiac letter enclosing a fragment from a bloody shirt. The writer complained of the inefficiency of the police, and went on: 'Schoolchildren make good targets. I think I shall wipe out a school bus one morning some time. Just shoot out the tyres, then pick off the kiddies as they come bouncing out.' Fortunately this threat was never carried out, but special security measures were taken by schools and school buses for some considerable time afterwards.

The murder of the cab-driver was the last known Zodiac killing. On 21 October a caller claiming to be the Zodiac killer rang the police at Oakland and declared that he would be willing to give himself up if he could be represented by a famous lawyer, his first choices being F. Lee Bailey and Melvin Belli. He also asked that he be allowed time on an early-morning talk show on TV. This was done, in an effort to apprehend him. Thousands of people in the area watched the Jim Dunbar show when it started at 6.45 a.m. At 7.41 a caller came on to the line, speaking in a soft, boyish voice, and identified himself as the Zodiac Killer. He called back fifteen times, and talked on the programme to Melvin Belli about his murders and about the blinding headaches from which he suffered. He ended by agreeing to meet Belli in front of a store in Daly City, but failed to keep the appointment.

Three people who had heard the Zodiac's voice, Bryan Hartnell, a woman telephone operator and a patrolman, said that the voice on the show bore no resemblance to the voice of the killer they had heard. On the other hand, two months after the show, Melvin Belli received a letter in the same handwriting as the letters received earlier by the newspapers. This letter enclosed another piece of the murdered cab-driver's shirt, and it claimed that the writer had killed eight people so far and soon intended to kill a ninth. If the caller on the television show had been an impostor, it would have been likely that the writer of the letter would have exposed him as the perpetrator of a hoax.

In March 1971 the *Los Angeles Times* received another letter, in which the writer said: 'If the blue menaces are ever going to catch me, they had better get off their fat butts and do something.' The letter concluded: 'The reason I am writing to the *Times* is so that they don't bury me on the back pages like some of the others.' This letter was signed with a cross surmounting a circle, and the number seventeen followed by a plus sign.

In 1974 the San Francisco Police Department received another letter from the Zodiac, claiming that he had now killed thirty-seven people and that he would 'do something nasty' unless he received more newspaper publicity. The police confirmed that the handwriting was identical to that of previous letters.

That letter was the last Zodiac communication received by any newspaper, police department or, as far as is known, anyone else, and the killings also stopped. It is very unlikely that he had in fact killed thirty-seven people, but it is possible that eleven or twelve could be ascribed to him, although there is no proof of any except the ones described in this account. But the police of the area which was Zodiac's stamping-ground are still fuming, because whether their officers were Gemini or Virgo, Aquarius or Pisces, Leo or Cancer, none of them could catch him.

# CHAPTER NINETEEN

## Manhunt for a Musician

A US Army sergeant and his girl friend, Margaret Harold, had parked their car at the side of the road just across the Maryland state line near Annapolis. The night of 26 June 1957 was unseasonably warm. They left the car for a breath of fresh air and drank a couple of beers from a six-pack that the sergeant had put into an iced container. Then they returned to their car and continued to drive along the road.

Soon afterwards they were overtaken by a speeding green Chrysler car, which swerved across ahead of them, forcing them to pull in and stop at the roadside. The driver of the Chrysler got out of his car and walked over to the sergeant's car, going round to the nearside. Leaning in at the open window on the passenger side, Margaret Harold nervously recoiled from this unexpected intrusion. 'What the hell do you want?' the sergeant demanded. As he said this he looked up, and saw the shining nickel plating of a .38 pistol only inches from his face.

The attacker then opened the rear door of the car and climbed in and pressed the muzzle of the pistol against the back of the driver's head. With his other hand he started to caress the back of the girl's neck and move his fingers up into her hair. The girl moved to try to avoid him and, predictably, this annoyed him. Moving the gun quickly, the attacker shot her in the face.

The Army sergeant knew that if he were to remonstrate with the intruder as he crouched over the girl where she had fallen sideways to the floor of the car, he would be shot.

181

That would not help anybody. If he tried to escape he would at least have a sporting chance of coming out of the situation alive and being able to describe the gunman to the police. Accordingly, he jumped from the car as the gunman was concentrating his attention on the girl, and ran as fast as he could along the road in the direction opposite to which he had been travelling. This was in order to minimize his chances of being shot in the back as he fled. He hoped to be able to stop an oncoming vehicle, but none appeared. He ran until he was out of breath – at least a mile. Near Route 450 he found a farmhouse where he asked permission to use the telephone to call police and an ambulance to go to the scene from which he had barely escaped with his life.

Police arrived to find the girl lying dead in the road with a hole in the side of her head and her hair matted with blood. The sergeant's car was just as he had left it, slewed into the roadside verge. The fingerprint detail went over the car from top to bottom but found no prints other than those of the driver, who was the owner of the car, and the dead woman. A thorough search was made of the surrounding area and not far away Police Chief William Wade and Lieutenant Hagner noted an unoccupied cinder-block building with a broken window, which they thought might be worthy of investigation. Managing to get inside, they discovered that this derelict building was apparently being used as a 'den' by someone. Pasted on all the interior walls in the basement, from top to bottom, were photographs – pin-ups, nudes, pornographic pictures cut from men's magazines and several photographs which did not seem to have any commercial connection but looked as if they might have been taken by the tenant of the 'den' with an instant-type camera such as a Polaroid.

The officers stared at this collection bug-eyed. Their gaze lighted upon a particular photograph which stood out from all the rest because it was of a girl fully-dressed among a sea of naked bodies. The girl, the officers noted, was very beautiful and they also noted, with commendable detachment, that the paper on which this particular photograph had been printed was not the kind normally used for the purpose. Wade removed this photograph from the wall and sent it to Washington for analysis at the FBI laboratory. Experts reported that the paper on which it had been printed was the kind generally used by college yearbook printers, and the Bureau checked all the colleges in the vicinity of Annapolis. Quite soon they were able to trace it to the University of Maryland. The photograph was that of a 1955 graduate named Wanda Tipson. When the FBI questioned her, however, she could not provide a single clue as to who could have her picture. The Army sergeant had described the killer of his girlfriend as a 'tall, thin-faced man with long hair', but none of the young graduate's dates fitted this description. It was a dead end as far as this aspect of the investigation was concerned.

The murder of Margaret Harold lay dormant in police files for a year and a half. Then, in the state of Virginia, another similar kind of attack took place, which led police to believe that the two could have been the work of the same man. On a night in January 1959 twenty-nine-year-old Carroll Jackson, a big, burly lorry-driver over six feet tall, was driving his wife Mildred home with their two young daughters, aged four years and eighteen months respectively, after a visit to relatives. Mildred was in the passenger seat of their car holding Janet, the baby, while Susan, the other child, sat in the rear seat. In order to reach his residence, Jackson had to switch from a main road to a subsidiary unmade-up dirt road, and as he was driving carefully along this road to avoid the numerous potholes, he was almost blinded by brilliant headlights from a car gradually creeping up behind him. Jackson had the impression that the driver was keeping these glaring headlights trained on his car deliberately so as to dazzle him.

When Jackson slowed his car, the other car did likewise, and this cat-and-mouse game was kept up for several miles. Jackson altered the position of his rear-view mirror so that he could see better what was going on, and at that point the car that was following him shot forward and came up alongside, keeping pace with him. Jackson, by now more annoyed than alarmed, decided to stop his car, get out and go over to the other driver and ask him what the hell he was playing at.

Seeing Jackson alighting from his vehicle, the tall, thin-faced man with long hair jumped from his car and ran towards him. Not only were his long locks waving in the wind, but also a nickel-plated .38 was waving in his right hand. With his other hand he motioned Jackson back to his car, following behind him closely, and when he reached Jackson's car he looked inside and saw Mildred and the two little girls. He ordered them all outside and told Jackson to turn out his headlights. Mildred carried the baby and helped Susan from the rear seat before walking over to where her husband was standing. Jackson then asked the gunman if he wanted their money. The man's reply, waving the gun menacingly, was, 'Shut up! All of you come over here and get into my car.'

Jackson kept his eyes trained on the gun, waiting for a suitable opportunity to knock it out of the man's hand and then knock him out with a well-aimed punch. No such chance offered itself and he had no choice but to obey the gunman's commands if he wanted to save the lives of himself and his family. The gunman removed Jackson's necktie and bound his hands with it; then he forced the entire family into the trunk of his car, leaving Jackson's car at the roadside. He then sped off along the isolated road.

The next day, Jackson's abandoned car was spotted by a relative, Mrs H.M. Ballard, not far from his home. She was somewhat puzzled that his car should have seemingly been left unattended in such an isolated place and she decided to call Sheriff Willis E. Proffitt. He immediately went to investigate and found the car keys still in the ignition, Mrs Jackson's handbag with the money inside it removed, and the children's toys on the rear seat of the car, but there was no sign of the family. In addition, there were skid marks directly in front of the car, which to the sheriff meant only one thing: the Jacksons had been forced to pull over by another car, the driver of which was most likely armed.

The county police, the local law enforcement officers and the FBI, working in collaboration, came up with nothing at all by way of a lead. The case seemed to come to a dead end.

Almost two months were to elapse before the fate of the Jackson family was revealed. On 4 March 1959 two men named James Beach and John Scott were driving near Fredericksburg, Virginia, when their car became bogged down in the mud. Beach left the car and went along the road looking for some brushwood to use as traction to enable them to pull the car clear. As he removed some wood he saw the legs of a dead man sticking out from the undergrowth. It was the body of Carroll Jackson.

Beach and his companion lost no time in getting their car out of the mud and drove off at speed to call the police. The dead man had been shot through the head at point-blank range. As the officers moved the body, they discovered the body of eighteen-month-old Janet beneath the corpse, and the subsequent autopsy showed that she had died from suffocation by having been placed under her father's dead body while she was still alive.

Two weeks or so after this discovery, two boys were playing near the cinder-block building near the site of the shooting of Margaret Harold. The boys thought they had found a gopher hole, so they started to remove earth from a small mound, hoping to uncover a gopher's nest. As they did so they saw the blonde hair of a little girl. They were so terrified that they dropped everything and never stopped running until they found a policeman.

Once again, the investigation was carried out under the leadership of Chief Wade and Lieutenant Hagner. Mildred Jackson was found under another mound of earth near where the boys had discovered little Susan buried. Susan had been bludgeoned to death with a blunt instrument, while Mildred had been strangled and beaten to death. It was not clear from the autopsy which had occurred first, so she could have died from strangulation or from the beating. The autopsy also revealed that she had been repeatedly raped before death, and the coroner stated that the sexual assault was one of the most brutal he had ever investigated. A red button was found in the basement of the cinder-block building which matched those on Mildred Jackson's dress, proving that she had been raped and killed there. Police were now sure that the killer of Margaret Harold and of the Jackson family were the same person.

The manhunt swung into action with intense publicity, which elicited several letters from people describing a man they had seen 'behaving in a weird manner' who drove either a blue or a green Ford. One letter, from a man in Norfolk, Virginia, proved to be the bombshell that cracked the case wide open. The writer of this letter accused a young musician named Melvin David Rees of the murders of Margaret Harold and the Jackson family. He said that he was a salesman, a friend of Rees, and that they had been together during the Harold slaying. He said that Rees was 'doped up to the eyeballs on speed' and had been acting in a wild, uncontrolled manner. He went on to say that he had asked Rees to his face whether he had killed the Jackson family, and that Rees, while he neither admitted nor denied it, had evaded the question. He described the musician as being tall, thin-faced, and having long hair.

Local police and the FBI checked out Rees's background, and pieces of the jigsaw now began to fit. In 1953 Rees had attended the University of Maryland, which went a long way towards explaining how he had been able to obtain the photograph of the co-ed Wanda Tipson to include in his pin-up gallery. On a check of police records, it was found that on 12 March 1955 Rees had been charged with assaulting a thirty-six-year-old woman and pulling her into his car when she refused to ride with him. Subsequently she had dropped the charges, so no more came of this incident.

The FBI spread their dragnet wider, but there were no

further leads until Rees's salesman friend received a letter from him postmarked West Memphis, Arkansas. FBI men closed in on the area and located Rees in a music store where he was employed as a piano salesman. Rees was taken into custody but he denied all knowledge of the murders. However, the Army sergeant who had seen Rees shoot his girl friend, picked him out of a police line-up without hesitation.

G-men who went to Rees's parents' home with a search warrant were rewarded by finding a .38 nickel-plated pistol hidden in the attic, under the lining of a saxophone case. The agents found also hidden in similar manner various notes written by Rees describing in detail his various crimes against women. There was also a newspaper photograph of Mildred Jackson clipped to a note about the killing, which read:

> Caught on a lonely road . . . After pulling them over, leveled pistol and ordered them out and into car trunk, which was opened by husband, and both bound. Drove to select area and killed husband and baby. Now the mother and daughter were all mine . . .

He then went on to describe the various perverted sex acts which he had forced Mrs Jackson to perform, concluding the account with the words, 'I was her master.' A postscript described how he had caused Mildred Jackson to undergo a slow, agonizing death which could only be described as a nightmare of sadism.

Other overwhelming evidence linked this berserk killer to the hitherto unsolved murders of four other girls. They were Mary Marie Shomette, sixteen; Ann Ryan, fourteen; Mary Elizabeth Fellers, eighteen, and Shelby Jean Venables, sixteen. The first two were both killed after being sexually assaulted in College Park, near the University of Maryland. The bodies of the last two, naked and mutilated, were found floating in Maryland rivers.

Rees faced trial in Baltimore in 1961 and was condemned

to life imprisonment. Unlike others similarly sentenced, the swinging musician was not going to get off with serving a term of life imprisonment followed by the usual parole for good behaviour. The State of Virginia also had claims upon him for murdering the Jackson family. For this he was sentenced to the same fate that he had so mercilessly meted out to nine other persons – death. The only difference was that his death in the electric chair was more humane than that suffered by his victims.

# CHAPTER TWENTY

## Where is Bible John?

The dance hall has always been a popular meeting-place for
Glasgow's lads and lasses. 'I met my wife at the dancing',
is a comment often heard from older Glaswegians. Only
recently has some of the magic of the dance hall declined
in the face of competition from discos, bingo, clubs and
other such meeting-places. One Glasgow dance hall, the
Barrowland, has always been particularly popular on
Thursday nights – from the sixties onwards, Thursday was
always 'Over-25s' night. Many of the patrons were better
dancers than their less experienced younger counterparts,
and many were married, although few brought their spouses
with them. It was thus that three young women looking for
a good time visited the Barrowland within a twenty-month
period, anticipating a night of dancing and fun. Little
did they know that this night out on the town was to
be their last.

In February 1968 Patricia Docker, twenty-five, who was
separated with a four-year-old son, shared a flat at 29
Langside Place, just around the corner from Glasgow
Infirmary, with her parents, John Wilson and his wife.
Patricia was employed as a nursing auxiliary at Mearnskirk
Hospital. Normally she worked the night shift from 10 p.m.
to 8 a.m. with every Tuesday, Wednesday and Thursday
off, when her mother took her place – a very convenient
arrangement from the babysitting angle. Patricia, who was
of medium height, slim, with short brown wavy hair, tip-
tilted nose and hazel eyes, was very keen on dancing and

189

on her free nights she attended the Locarno, the Majestic or the Barrowland.

On Thursday, 22 February 1968, she told her parents that she was going to the Majestic in Hope Street. Here, too, Thursday was always an 'over-25s' night and certain to be crowded to capacity. Wearing a yellow wool dress, a grey duffle coat with a blue fur collar, brown shoes, and carrying a brown handbag, she left home about half-way through the evening. Her family would never see her again alive.

The following morning Maurice Goodman, of 27 Carmichael Place, was walking the few yards from his home around the corner into Carmichael Lane, where he kept his car in a lock-up garage. As he reached the recess at the garage door, he jumped back with shock. A woman's naked body lay crumpled in the doorway.

Mr Goodman did not hang around. Horror-stricken, he rushed from the scene to call the police. The information was flashed to the Flying Squad at Glasgow Central Police Office. Detective Sergeant Andrew Johnstone and Detective Constable Norman MacDonald were first on the scene. Immediately they realized that this would mark the start of a major inquiry, for it appeared highly improbable that this was a natural death.

A squad of officers was assembled under the personal supervision of Detective Chief Superintendent Elphinstone Dalglish. The first task was to establish the cause of death and the victim's identity. The former was the job of the police surgeon, Dr James Imrie, who arrived soon afterwards. He discovered that the principal injuries were ligature marks on the neck, which suggested manual strangulation, and that she had been strangled with something strong, such as a leather belt. There were also facial and head injuries of a type consistent with punching or kicking, or both, but none of these would have caused her death. Ascertaining the time of death was more difficult – not only was the body stiffened with the onset of *rigor mortis* but also with frost.

While the police squad started house-to-house inquiries,

an improvised shelter was erected around the body to enable forensic experts to comb the immediate area for clues. One was found immediately: a soiled sanitary pad. It seemed likely that the girl had been menstruating at the time of her death, and this was later confirmed at the post-mortem.

A woman living nearby said that she had heard a female voice shouting 'Leave me alone!' during the previous night. She could not pinpoint the time. An ambulanceman said he was sure he recognized the victim as a nurse: the police made an immediate check. No nurses were reported missing at any hospitals in the area, although it was difficult to be certain because the staff worked different shifts, and in any event some were on leave. Various passers-by were questioned, but they could not help. Searches of the area revealed no further clues, nor anything which could identify the body, and by lunch-time on Friday it had been removed to the police mortuary. Still they wondered: 'Who was she?'

The body acquired the name of Patricia Docker late on Friday evening when her father heard that the body of an unidentified young woman had been found only yards from his own home. He then contacted the police immediately and identified her. He had not, he told police, been overly concerned when Patricia had not returned home after the dance on Thursday night because she often stayed overnight with a girl friend on such occasions.

The autopsy was performed by Professor Gilbert Forbes of the Department of Forensic Medicine at Glasgow University and confirmed Dr Imrie's earlier findings – it was clearly a case of manual strangulation. There was no clear evidence of sexual assault. Now that the police knew the cause of death and the identity of the victim, they could start looking in earnest for the killer. Where had the girl been before she was killed? Had anyone seen her? Did anyone have a motive for killing her? The police theory was that she had probably met her killer for the first time at the dance hall and had gone willingly with him to the place where she was found. Most likely she had refused him sexual favours because she was having her period and he had killed her in frustrated rage. The police, however, were wary of speculation; what they needed were hard facts.

On being informed by Patricia's parents that she had told them she was going to the Majestic Ballroom in Hope Street the inquiry switched to this establishment. That same night, policemen and women went to the dance – not, however, with the idea of joining in the fun. What they wanted to find out was whether anyone had seen Patricia there the previous night and, above all, was she with someone and, if so, whom? Had the girl been seen leaving the hall with a particular person? If so, did the patrons know him – in other words, was he a regular?

When police arrive at a dance hall it is usually because of fighting or trouble with drugs. But on that Friday night the several hundred dancers were startled to find police officers on the bandstand and an announcement was made over the tannoy that anyone who had been in the ballroom the previous night should go to the foyer immediately. A surprising number did so. They were shown a photograph of Patricia Docker and asked whether they had seen her the previous evening. Meanwhile, police were still searching the area intensively for Patricia's missing clothes and handbag. Her clothing was never found, though her handbag and part of the casing of her watch were eventually recovered from the nearby River Cart by police frogmen. However, these items provided no clues.

A reliable lead next surfaced to the effect that Patricia had not been dancing at the Majestic at all but at the Barrowland. Apparently she had changed her mind, possibly having met a girl friend who was headed for the Barrowland and decided to accompany her. The whole inquiry now switched to the Barrowland. If the checks at the Majestic had been fruitless, this time it was like looking for a needle in the proverbial haystack. When officers approached the patrons for information, nobody knew, nor wanted to know. Patricia had been there on a Thursday, the night when men and women did not always use their real names, or let their family or friends know where they were. Police offered to preserve the anonymity of any persons who came forward, at the same time indicating that if they said anything material to the case this anonymity would have to be waived. The result was a complete blank. Detective Chief Superintendent Dalglish and his colleagues were stymied, they had nothing to go on. The inquiry slowly wound down, though the file remained open. The police knew only one thing for sure: there was a killer loose on the streets of Glasgow.

Bridgeton Cross is the meeting-place of many thoroughfares leading to all parts of the city. A few yards off Main Street lies Mackeith Street. At No.15 lived a thirty-two-year-old mother of three named Jemima McDonald, with Elizabeth, twelve, Andrew, nine and Alan, seven, just across the landing from her sister, Mrs Margaret O'Brien. Margaret often kept an eye on Jemima's children while she was out, for Jemima and her children constituted what is now called a single-parent family, separated but not divorced. Like Patricia Docker, Jemima enjoyed dancing and frequented many of the same places, especially the Barrowland, barely half a mile away, particularly on Thursdays and at week ends. Saturday, 16 August 1969 was her final visit, for it was to be the last night of her life. As with Patricia Docker, a night's dancing was to be the prelude to a violent death.

When Jemima did not return home that Saturday night she was not particularly missed. Her sister, who was looking after her children, did not worry, because this was not unusual for her. Throughout the next day, a hot summer Sunday, children played in the streets, including Jemima's own three children. A little way from Mackeith Street stood some derelict tenements and it was there that a grim find was soon made. Some small children were overheard by a neighbour to say something about 'a body in a building'. At first no one took much notice; after all, it was not at all uncommon for down-and-out dossers or alcoholics to sleep off the stupor of a Saturday night in an unoccupied house. The children's chatter was so persistent, however, that when on Monday morning Jemima had still not returned home, her sister Margaret became apprehensive. Remembering what she had heard the children saying all the previous day, she made her way to the derelict flats at 23 Mackeith Street and started exploring them. There she found Jemima's body, partly-clothed. She had been strangled with her own tights.

At about 10 a.m. on that August morning Margaret O'Brien rushed shrieking from the building to raise the alarm. It was soon to transpire that Jemima's body had lain there for at least thirty hours.

The inquiry into Jemima McDonald's death was spearheaded by Detective Chief Superintendent Thomas Goodall, head of Glasgow CID. It was to be his last murder case, a few weeks later he was to fall victim to a longstanding heart condition. At first the police did not link the death of Jemima McDonald with that of Patricia Docker, but when it was discovered that Jemima had been dancing at the Barrowland on the night of her death, further coincidences began to emerge. Both murders had been committed in the same manner, and both victims were young women. When it was found that Jemima's handbag was missing, police remembered the search for Patricia Docker's missing handbag and clothing. Corporation dustmen arrived at Mackeith Street to sift through the mounds of rubbish piled indiscriminately in backyards, but Jemima's handbag was never found. And when the autopsy had been performed on Jemima's body, another weird coincidence surfaced – like Patricia, Jemima had been menstruating at the time of her death. Did this have any bearing on the murder? A chilling thought entered the minds of the police. Were they seeking some kind of sex deviate? One with a hang-up about menstruation?

Police quickly established that Jemima had been dancing at the Barrowland on the Saturday night and appealed for information with her description: five feet seven inches tall, slim build, dark brown hair with fair streaks. She had been wearing a black dress, a white frilly blouse and white high-heeled slingback shoes. Almost immediately leads began to come in. She had been seen by people at the dance who were able to fill in some details of her last movements. She had almost certainly left the Barrowland just after midnight with an unknown man. She had been seen in Bain Street near the ballroom, then walking along the London Road either to Main Street or to Landressy Street, just yards from Bridgeton Cross, near her home in Mackeith Street, arriving there at about 1 a.m. on the Sunday morning. Once more police descended on the Barrowland. Teams of detectives spoke to all the dancers, while Jemima's picture was flashed on a screen with a full description of her last known movements.

This time, a week after the murder, the police had sufficient information to enable them to put together a picture of the person they wanted to interview. The suspect was described as being between twenty-five and thirty-five years old, between six feet and six feet two inches tall, of slim build, with reddish fair hair worn in a neat short style, and wearing a good quality suit with a white shirt. This description had been pieced together principally with the help of two witnesses, a boy and a girl, each of whom thought they had seen Jemima with a man of that description on the evening in question. The boy had seen them sitting in a pub, while the girl had seen them sitting together on a seat in the Barrowland. Since neither had felt confident about putting together an Identikit picture for the police, the latter looked for another way of transforming their description into a visual record – perhaps a professional artist could help. On the suggestion of another senior officer, Detective Superintendent James Binnie approached the Glasgow School of Art in the hope that someone there might be able to assist. The deputy director, Lennox Paterson, agreed to work with the police in composing a likeness. The police took the two witnesses, who did not know each other, to the art school, where Paterson interviewed them separately. The boy confirmed some of the details given by the girl. Paterson's drawing resembled a soft-focus photograph with just sufficient clarity to enable someone to recognize the person depicted and both witnesses said that the finished drawing strongly resembled the suspect. Lennox Paterson's portrait appeared in newspapers and on television throughout Scotland. It was the first real break the police had had and at last they now had something to go on. With a face to show possible witnesses, the door-to-door inquiries and the checking of dancers took on a new significance. Police efforts at the Barrowland intensified. Male and female officers attended in plain clothes, looking out for the suspect. Once the initial hue and cry had subsided, perhaps the killer might return to his former scene of operations.

Throughout those first few weeks police activity was intense. All the standard techniques were employed, including a reconstruction of that Saturday night's events. A policewoman wearing clothing similar to that worn by Jemima McDonald retraced her last walk from the Barrowland to Mackeith Street, in the hope that seeing her would jog someone's memory. She was discreetly shadowed by a small team of detectives who would note any information received, but this drew a blank. However, the fact that people saw overt police activity on the streets would again remind them that a brutal murder had been committed and that a huge inquiry was on their very doorstep.

Jemima's family put up a reward of £100 for anyone who could give the police information leading to the apprehension of her killer. The reward was never claimed. One sister refused to disclose her address to the media, terrified that the killer might come after her.

Slowly information stopped filtering in and police activity dwindled. Another comparison with the Patricia Docker case had become apparent: there was not going to be an arrest in the foreseeable future. Public attention was diverted by other things. Then Detective Chief Superintendent Thomas Goodall dropped dead of a heart attack and the case passed under the control of Detective Superintendent James Binnie of Glasgow's Eastern Division. Towards the end of

October 1969 the police stopped their activities at the Barrowland. Unknown to James Binnie and his colleagues, this was a fateful decision. But they could hardly do otherwise, considering their notable lack of success. They had already made themselves highly unpopular with the regular clientele and the dramatic drop in attendance figures was catastrophic. The management made it clear that the police presence was no longer welcome. And so, slowly, the crowds started to return.

Two unsolved murders of women in eighteen months. On the surface the night-life of Glasgow continued, little affected after all that time. Any thought of murder, if it existed at all, was pushed into the background. The social habits of Glaswegians die hard.

Thus it was with Helen Puttock, a twenty-nine-year-old mother of two from Scotstoun. Helen, too, loved dancing. Married to George Puttock, a soldier in the REME, she had a wide circle of friends and was very popular and sociable. George had no objection to her visiting the Barrowland with her girlfriends. He looked upon her dancing craze with amused tolerance, and willingly babysat their two children on Thursday nights. So he expressed no surprise when Helen, on Thursday, 30 October 1969, announced that she would be going to the Barrowland for a night out with her sister Jeannie.

That night Jeannie called for Helen at about 7 p.m. and waited for her to get ready. Helen was an attractive girl, five feet eight inches tall, a brunette. She chose a short black dress with short sleeves, black shoes, and an imitation ocelot fur coat. She carried a black purse. Jeannie wore a blouse and skirt and a dark green coat with a sheepskin collar. They had arranged to meet two other girls, Marion Cadder and Jean O'Donnell, before going on to the dance hall. George saw them off at about 8.30 p.m. and gave his sister-in-law some money for a cab to get home, since the buses would be no longer running by that time. The two girls caught a bus in nearby Dumbarton Road to take them into town. Their route took them past the shipyards and wharves of the Clyde, through Partick with its tenements blackened with the grime of ages, past the Kelvin Hall and Art Gallery, into the city centre. The bus reached Glasgow Cross at about 9 p.m. and Helen and Jeannie alighted into the milling throng, for the streets were still busy around this famous Glasgow landmark. They knew that the ballroom would not be full until about 10 p.m. and would not be much fun early on, so they went in search of a drink, like most of the patrons. The area was certainly not short of pubs and the girls chose the Traders' Tavern in Kent Street. It was crowded not only with locals but also with many others who would be going on to the dance hall. This was 1969, when pubs closed at 10 p.m.

Helen and Jeannie left the pub just before closing-time, having met their friends Marion Cadder and Jean O'Donnell there as arranged. Arriving at the Barrowland, the girls left their coats in the cloakroom and headed for the floor. The hall was very crowded; the atmosphere was electric. The noise from the band boomed out over the heads of the crowd. Couples gyrated wildly, while the unattached but hopeful thronged the sides of the hall. Soon Jeannie was asked for a dance by a man who said his name was John. Like Jeannie herself, John was a very good dancer and they soon decided to stay together on the floor for the rest of the evening. He told Jeannie he came from Castlemilk and that he was a roofer. She felt pretty sure that he was a married man.

Jeannie first became aware of the person who was to change her life when she saw a man leaning against a pillar to the side of the hall. As Helen passed within range of him, he asked her to dance, and they were soon whirling round the floor. At a break in the music the two couples met, and Helen introduced her partner. 'This is John,' she said. 'So you're John, too!' answered Jeannie. 'My partner's John as well. It seems everyone around here is called John!' The two couples stayed together for the rest of the evening, pausing to chat between dances.

Helen's partner was not the usual Barrowland type, Jeannie was to say later. Many of the patrons were rough-necks and as often as not drunk. This chap was polite and well-mannered, and softly-spoken: so much so, in fact that he stuck out like a sore thumb. He was tall, about five feet ten inches, and aged between twenty-five and thirty-five. He had reddish-tinged sandy hair, cropped fairly short and rounded neatly at the back. Longer hair being fashionable at the time, his hairstyle alone distinguished him. He had a well-scrubbed, boyish look. Jeannie also noticed that his two front teeth overlapped slightly, and one tooth was missing. He wore a well-cut brown suit with a blue shirt and a dark tie with thin red stripes across it, rather like a military or old school tie. Helen seemed to enjoy his company, for they laughed and joked together. Jeannie observed, too, that when Helen came to sit and rest between dances John would pull out her chair for her. Jeannie was amazed, for this kind of chivalry was almost unknown in Barrowland circles.

Eventually, at 11.30 p.m., the band played its last number and the two couples retrieved their coats. As they were leaving the hall, John (Helen's partner) made a remark which would remain in Jeannie's memory and which she was to recall later: 'My father says these places are dens of iniquity.' Jeannie was too surprised to reply.

The two couples headed for Glasgow Cross where there was a cab rank and the two girls eventually commandeered a cab. 'What are you going to do now?' (Helen's) John said to Jeannie's escort. 'It's OK,' he replied, 'I'm going to George Square to get the all-night bus.' 'See you around,' Jeannie said. 'Cheerio for now.' Turning to Helen, she asked her about *her* John. 'Is he seeing us home or what? Where does he come from?' 'Haven't the foggiest,' replied Helen as John entered the cab with the two girls and it set off.

Jeannie's phenomenal memory for details was particularly good regarding a number of matters which were later to assume great significance. John was broody and aloof, and when asked a direct question he either changed the subject or ignored it altogether – quite a contrast to his erstwhile good manners. To Helen he appeared to be annoyed that Jeannie was in the cab with them and he made no attempt to hide this. Conversation was therefore somewhat stilted but some aspects of it were quite unusual, to say the least. Jeannie recalled later how John had said that he disapproved of married women going to dances and spoke generally of 'adulterous women'. When asked what he did at Hogmanay, he said he did not drink, but prayed. John then went on to talk about the Bible, discoursing on the subject of Moses and his laws, going on to talk about a woman who had been taken in adultery and stoned, and another woman who had been standing by a well. It was later, when the police were hunting for this elusive unknown man, that he acquired his nickname of 'Bible John'.

As the cab drew into Earl Street, John insisted that Jeannie should alight first and walk the remaining short distance to her home. John then directed the driver to continue on his way. By this time Jeannie was very clear in her own mind that John had been very much put out by her presence and obviously wanted to get Helen alone. 'Maybe I'll see you next week,' she said as she alighted. John did not reply. What a rude fellow, she thought to herself. His good manners in the dance-hall had been a sham. The cab then turned and sped back towards Earl Street.

What happened afterwards is not known. It was the last time that Helen was seen alive, but not quite the last time anyone saw her weird dancing-partner. At about 2 a.m. on Friday morning the night service bus picked up a dishevelled-looking man in Dumbarton Road. A passenger noticed that the stranger had a livid red mark on his cheek just below the eye, and also that his jacket was very muddy. The significance of this was lost on the passenger at the time, but he was almost certainly looking at a murderer, who at the junction of Dumbarton Road and Gray Street alighted and disappeared. He has never been seen since.

Archie MacIntyre, a forty-year-old Glasgow Corpora
Highways Department road worker, came out of his
tenement flat at 95 Earl Street at 7 a.m. on Friday, 31
October 1969, to take his dog for a walk. The dog started
sniffing and whining round the back of the tenement and
Archie went to take a closer look. He saw what looked like
a bundle of rags lying beside a drainpipe. 'When I got
closer,' recalled Archie, 'I got the shock of my life. I saw
it was a woman's body, and it was a funny colour. She had
a fur coat on. I didn't stop to look any further, I just ran
back to the Close.' He then dashed to a public call-box and
dialled 999. 'Get the police!' he gasped. He was immediately
connected and agitatedly described his discovery. Within
minutes, even before Archie had reached his home, two
ambulancemen and two constables had arrived. One of the
ambulancemen examined the crumpled figure huddled
against the wall. 'She's dead,' he said.

It required no great feat of detection to rule out both
accident and suicide. This was a case of murder right from
the start, for the cause of death was around the woman's
neck. She had been strangled with one of her own stockings.
The constables radioed for assistance from B Division at
Partick Police Station, and the senior officer on duty there
contacted Detective Superintendent Joe Beattie, and also
arranged for the head of Glasgow CID, Detective Chief
Superintendent Elphinstone Dalglish, and Detective
Superintendent James Binnie, to attend from the Central
Division. Beattie, a highly experienced officer who had been
in command of many past murder inquiries, immediately
assumed charge of the whole case. In less time than it takes
to tell they had all arrived at the scene, together with
the police doctor, photographer, fingerprint expert and,
in Scotland, the Procurator-Fiscal, whose duty is simply
to attend and check that the police have taken all the
initial steps.

The dead girl was fully-clothed, but her clothing was in
disarray. Grass and weeds had been caught between the soles

...er shoes. There was bruising to the face, ...had been struck by her assailant. A curious ...now surfaced: she, like the previous two ...been menstruating at the time of her death. ...y pad, however, was not in place; instead, it had ...tucked neatly under her armpit. Was this the work of some madman, the police wondered? There was no immediate evidence of sexual assault, but confirmation of that would have to await the autopsy. The police, however, were already remembering the names of Patricia Docker and Jemima McDonald, who had both been found strangled after a night at the Barrowland, and it had been 'that time of the month' for both of them, too. Was this the work of the same man? Beattie thought it was too early to voice this possibility, but the weird coincidences in all three cases were too obvious to ignore.

Signs of a struggle were found on the grass at the foot of the railway embankment behind the buildings. The ground was disturbed, as though there had been a chase. It appeared that the girl had tried to escape her attacker's attentions by scrambling up the bank and had reached halfway before being overpowered, after which she had been punched on the head to stun her and then had been dragged back across the grass, her heels catching in the long strands. Near the rear wall of the tenement the killer had removed a stocking from her inert body, strangled her and left her body against the wall.

The doctor could not be certain as to the exact time of death, but she had been dead for some hours. Archie MacIntyre did not know her, and the body carried no identification papers; once again, her handbag was missing. The mystery, however, was soon solved. George Puttock, who lived only a few hundred yards away at 129 Earl Street, had heard the commotion and seen the flurry of police activity. His wife had not returned home the previous night from the dance; he had assumed she had stayed at her sister's, which she had done many times before on these occasions, so he had not given it much thought. But on seeing the police he walked towards them and told them that his wife had not returned home. Immediately Joe Beattie took him to the back of the building and showed him the body, which George identified immediately. Thus started the biggest manhunt in Scottish criminal history. Neither Archie MacIntyre nor the other residents of Earl Street were to get any peace that day, nor for weeks afterwards. The whole panoply of a major police investigation swung into action. Shattering the early-morning calm, a squad of detectives started their door-to-door inquiries.

Jeannie, as a prime witness, was interviewed by Joe Beattie personally. It was but the first of countless interviews and meetings between them over the following years. Joe quickly discovered that Jeannie had a prodigious memory for small details. Within a few hours Jeannie was working out with the police an Identikit picture of 'Bible John'.

It so happened that on one of Jeannie's visits to police headquarters she saw on the office wall the drawing by Lennox Paterson of the Jemima McDonald suspect, and without any prompting or prior knowledge Jeannie immediately cried, 'That man looks just like him!' This shook the murder squad, for only they knew of the similarities between the deaths of Jemima McDonald and Helen Puttock, and now here was a witness who had almost certainly been with the killer of Helen Puttock saying that he looked like the prime suspect in the McDonald case two months earlier! Beattie's immediate reaction was to ask Paterson to draw an impression of the Puttock case suspect from Jeannie's detailed description. Paterson took three days, deciding to do a colour painting. The result, when shown to Jeannie, confirmed the wildest hopes of the police. 'That's him!' she cried. Prints were made up as posters, and the similarity between this painting and Paterson's drawing of the McDonald suspect convinced the police that the same man was responsible for both murders – and that of Patricia Docker, too.

With three murders, probably connected, there was the truly frightening possibility that the killer might strike again. The suspect's pictures were circulated in every newspaper. Police also appealed for Jeannie's partner, 'Castlemilk John', as he came to be known, to come forward. But, like Bible John himself, he too had vanished from the scene. Many thousands of calls were received from other people – the public response was unprecedented. 'I've just seen Bible John getting off a bus,' someone would say. Or 'My neighbour goes to the Barrowland regularly. He looks rather like Bible John to me.' All these calls were followed up. Jeannie attended more than 300 identity parades, on countless occasions being brought from her place of employment at Maclaren Controls in West Street. Surprisingly, her employers accepted this with a good grace. However, none of the men Jeannie looked at was Bible John.

Dentists were asked to search their records for anyone with two overlapping front incisors and a missing tooth in the right upper jaw; this signified that Bible John had his own teeth and not dentures. No success resulted from this line of inquiry, nor from the police visits to over 450 men's hairdressers asking them if they recognized the suspect's picture with its distinctive haircut. Laundries and cleaners were also visited, rubbish tips and dustbins searched, ships were rigorously gone over with a fine tooth comb. All these efforts proved fruitless; Bible John still eluded them. Finally, the BBC showed a half-hour documentary on 18 September 1970, an evocative piece of teamwork presented by Hugh Cochrane and the BBC Research Team. Hugh Cochrane appealed to Bible John to give himself up, concluding with an apt quotation from Jeremiah, Chapter 23, Verse 24: 'Can any hide himself in secret places, that I shall not see him? saith the Lord.' The programme, followed up by vigorous Press campaigns, drew an encouraging public response – more than 200 calls were received. All were checked out, all led nowhere.

It is now seventeen years since the murder of Patricia Docker sparked off the greatest manhunt in Glasgow's history. Neither her death nor that of Jemima McDonald or Helen Puttock is any nearer a solution. Only one question now remains – *where is Bible John?*

If Bible John is still alive today, he would now be somewhere between forty-two and fifty-two years old. A person's appearance can change a good deal in seventeen years and being an egocentric type of individual, it is likely that he is living quite openly somewhere, relying on his changed appearance for protection. But what of his dark impulses? Has he managed to conquer his lust for killing? Or has he found that the relief of his inner tensions brought about by his crimes were merely transitory? In short, has he killed again? Could other murders committed elsewhere in Scotland be ascribed to him? After all, as we have seen in many of the preceding cases described in this book, many multiple murderers go on killing until they are caught. There is usually some character or personality defect which is recurrent, or some situation which is sufficient to spark off in the killer the compulsive need to murder. Let us look at some possibilities.

The following unsolved murders of young women in Scotland relate to 1977 onwards, which tends to suggest that if Bible John was responsible, he had either laid low for eight years or had been in some kind of situation which prevented him from committing murder.

After a night out on 5 August 1977 Anna Kenny, from the Gorbals in Glasgow, left the Hurdy-Gurdy Bar in Lister Street, Townhead, in the company of a girlfriend to look for a cab. It was believed she was offered a lift, but nothing more was heard of her until her body was found by a shepherd sixteen months later on 24 April 1979, at Skipness, Kintyre. The site of her grave, known as Rockfield, is a regular campsite for gypsies and tinkers. Police were baffled that the killer should have chosen such a site, for it is a very busy spot in summer, frequented not only by the travelling folk but also well-known as a lovers' trysting-place, whereas between Skipness and Arrochar there are miles of lonely uninhabited moorland where a body could have been buried and probably never discovered. However, as is well known, many multiple murderers have a compulsion to leave the bodies of their victims in a place public enough to ensure that they will be found in due course − Bible John's known three victims were all found within forty-eight hours, two having been left in full view.

Current police thinking is that Anna was picked up by a lorry-driver and driven to the site where she was found. A spade had been used to bury the body, and a spade is frequently carried by lorry-drivers to dig their vehicles out of snowdrifts or mud. Beyond the bare facts and this theory, nothing more is known of the circumstances of Anna's death and no one has been charged with her murder. Nor is there anything else particular to connect it with Bible John, beyond the fact that it appears to have been a chance killing and sexually motivated.

Striking comparisons, however, can be drawn between the killings attributed to Bible John and the murder of Hilda McAulay, a thirty-six-year-old divorced mother-of-two who lived in Drumlaken Street, Maryhill, Glasgow. She lived quietly, being naturally shy and reserved. Her one night out each week was a regular Saturday visit to a dance hall with a girlfriend, while her two children were looked after by their grandmother. On Saturday, 1 October 1977, she went to the Plaza Dance Hall in Glasgow with girlfriends. As usual, they went for a drink beforehand at McNee's Bar adjoining the Plaza, where she was seen in the company of a man aged thirty to thirty-five, tall and of slim build. She was seen at the dance just after midnight. The next morning her ravaged body was found in a lovers' lane at Westferry Caravan Site near Langbank in Renfrewshire by some boys who were out blackberrying. The body was almost naked and items of clothing were scattered in the bushes. She had been strangled.

Initially the police put out a call for the driver of a van which had been seen parked without lights between 4 and 6 a.m. near the scene of the murder. This driver came forward and, after questioning, he was eliminated. No other information provided any clues, but the officer in charge, Detective Superintendent Douglas Meldrum of Paisley CID, adopted a similar inquiry technique to that which had been followed by Joe Beattie eight years earlier. Three policewomen, Detective Constable Caroline Sneddon, Nancy Robertson and Sandra Harris, were all sent to the Plaza in plain clothes, but they drew a complete blank, although police are almost certain that Hilda met her murderer there. The story is depressingly like that of Helen Puttock. This case too is unsolved and many detectives think it may have been the work of Bible John.

Equally horrific, from the opposite side of the country, is the case of Christine Eadie and Helen Scott, two seventeen-year-olds whose bodies were found in East Lothian only two weeks later, on 16 October 1977. They were last seen alive the previous evening leaving the World's End pub in Edinburgh's High Street. Police think that they were in the company of two men and that the girls got into their car – a fatal decision, for both were to be strangled and beaten with their hands tied behind their backs. Despite the most extensive inquiry by Lothians and Borders Police, this case is still no nearer a solution. The only comparison, however, with the Bible John murders is that both girls were strangled and sexually assaulted.

Just two months later another unsolved case cropped up on Bible John's own territory. This was the case of Agnes Cooney, a twenty-three-year-old from Coatbridge, who was killed on 3 December 1977. She worked as a houseparent in a children's home in Bellshill, Lanarkshire. Early on the morning of 4 December 1977 John Stewart, a farm labourer at Crossrigg Farm found her body near Snipe Road, Caldercruix, Lanarkshire. She had been stabbed and battered to death. The body had lain there some hours, for Agnes's suède boots were covered with frost. There were heavy bloodstains nearby, indicating that the killing had occurred there. Once she had been identified, police discovered that she had spent the previous afternoon flat-hunting; then, at night, with her friend Gina Barclay, she had gone to the

Clada Club, not far from the Plaza Dance Hall. This was Agnes's first night out for months – she loved her job and did not go out much at all, and had no steady boyfriend. She was last seen alive just after midnight on Friday, 2 December 1977, at the Clada Club, and was believed to have left there alone. Police subsequently surmised that she had hitched a lift to Victoria Road or Cathcart Road and was probably driven to the city centre, from which she would have walked to the motorway slip road and hitched another lift to Coatbridge. Agnes, a regular hitchhiker, was known to use this route. The police put out a call for anyone who was in the vicinity and, indeed, anyone else who had been picked up by a driver offering a lift. They interviewed all the patrons of the Clada Club, but all these efforts came to nothing. Was this the work of Bible John? It was not his MO, for Agnes was stabbed, not strangled.

As if this were not enough, another girl from Glasgow was found murdered on 20 November 1978. She was seventeen-year-old Mary Gallacher from Springburn, whose body was found near Barnhill Station, Springburn. She had left her home the previous Sunday night on her way to meet friends and spend a few hours at a local club. She never met them, but met her killer instead. Very little more is known. As with all the others, the trail has gone dead and no arrest has been made. But the similarity to the other cases is there . . . a young girl, a chance meeting after a night out at a place of entertainment, a sexual murder, and the complete and utter disappearance of the killer.

Was Mary Gallacher the most recent victim of one man's lust for killing? Without more evidence, it is impossible to answer this question. Police files may officially remain open forever, but it would seem that Bible John is destined to go the same way as Jack the Ripper, who was never caught, and whose name has now passed into legend. One thing, however, is certain: if Bible John is still alive, the words of the prophet Isaiah will haunt him to the end of his days – 'There is no peace, saith the Lord, unto the wicked.'